BASIC ECCLESIAL
COMMUNITIES:
THE EVANGELIZATION OF THE POOR

ALVARO BARREIRO, S.J.

BASIC ECCLESIAL COMMUNITIES: THE EVANGELIZATION OF THE POOR

*Translated from the Portuguese
by Barbara Campbell*

BIP-90

ORBIS BOOKS

Maryknoll, New York 10545

Originally published as *Comunidades Eclesiais de Base e Evangelização dos Pobres,* copyright © 1977 by Edições Loyola, São Paulo, Brazil

English translation copyright © 1982 by Orbis Books, Maryknoll, NY 10545

Unless otherwise indicated, all biblical quotations have been taken from the New English Bible

---

Library of Congress Cataloging in Publication Data

Barreiro, Alvaro.
   Basic ecclesial communities.

   Translation of: Comunidades eclesiais de base e evangelização dos pobres.
   Includes bibliographical references.
   1. Christian communities—Catholic Church.
2. Christian communities—Brazil. 3. Church and the poor. 4. Evangelistic work. I. Title.
BX 2347.72.B6B3713   253   81-16898
ISBN 0-88344-026-1 (pbk.)   AACR2

CONTENTS

v

PREFACE

We cannot fail to be encouraged by the fact that the theologian's eyes are being turned with insight and love toward the evangelical poor—the wealth of the Basic Ecclesial Communities: poor, because they are fragile creatures born under the strong inspiration of the Spirit of God; wealth, because, in their newness, they stem from the ancient, venerable framework of the Church. They are ecclesial communities; they live in the spirit of the Church; they grow within the great universal community. However, they call themselves "basic," reminding us of the beginnings of evangelization by the Apostles, in the footsteps of the Great Master, Jesus.

Fr. Barreiro observes: "When the good news is preached to the poor, in a pure, free, and fearless manner, it kindles in them the fire of hope, transforming their lives." This book attempts to penetrate the mystery of this life born of the people, and this Church emerging from the base, not through an arbitrary human invention, but rather through the Spirit of God, which lies at the source of all life. Anyone who reads this work will become a little more aware of the evangelical wealth hidden in those small living cells of the Church which are, auspiciously, multiplying in Brazil and throughout our entire continent.

It should always be stressed that this new life has not cropped up by way of a dispute, but rather as an appeal for the conversion of all of us. It is precisely inherent in the Spirit of God to strike us with the evidence of God's gift against the self-sufficient egoism of our security. Hence, it should not be considered odd that one hears fearful and even slanderous statements made, out of dread that the poor weakness of those communities may prove excessively eloquent in its criticism of a Church marked by power, compromise, and conservatism, a criticism that is not made in words, nor in writing. Those communities are too poor, and feel too defenseless, moreover, to be concerned with polemics. It is the criticism of example, of the new practice of charity, of faith in the force of the Spirit and of the gospel, and of hope in the infinite, merciful grace of God.

We are happy to observe the author of this book pointing with such great insight, in the footsteps of serious exegetes, to the biblical origin of God's predilection for the poor. He attempts to make the matter transcend self-interested ideological polemics, and underscores the nucleus of the long-standing tradition of Scripture. The force of this text lies precisely in its sound scriptural foundation, nevertheless disarming us with the persuasive power of the Word of God. It is not a matter of defending our pastoral tastes and predilections, but rather of perceiving in Scripture, as a throbbing of the heart of God, the side toward which it is inclined, and then, in an effort at fidelity to revelation, making our affection and options incline toward the same side as well.

The author does not remain in a merely abstract and generic area. He tries to make his biblical reflection aid us in understanding the concrete reality of our Church. Thus, the examples that he cites from life in a concrete Basic Ecclesial Community, such as that of São Félix, show us more succinctly how the good news of the liberation of the human being proclaimed by Jesus has become a reality. The author concludes that the presence of the Basic Communities has ended up being an evangelization for the Church as a whole. The reflections set forth in this book will, unquestionably, lead us to a vision of greater hope in this Church which has been born of the people, through the force of the Spirit of God. In this respect, the reading of Fr. Barreiro's work will prove useful to all those of us who are experiencing this time of ecclesial birth, so as to understand it with greater theological discernment. For, as we read at the end of the book, it is only through "fidelity to the Spirit, who consecrated and sent the Messiah to evangelize the poor, that the Church can give witness to human beings of the good news of which it is the bearer and servant, at the command of its Lord." And this is happening, supernaturally, in the small basic ecclesial cells, in the poor sections of the rural areas and on the outskirts of the large cities. "I thank thee, Father, Lord of heaven and earth, for hiding these things from the learned and wise, and revealing them to the simple" (Luke 10:21).

J. B. LIBANIO, S.J.

FOREWORD TO THE ENGLISH TRANSLATION

There are real indications that the dramatic renewal of the Church in Latin America is making itself felt in the universal Church and specifically in the North American Catholic community. Three realities—all rooted in the socio-economic, political, and cultural complexities of Latin America—are powerfully contributing to a reawakening of consciences and a deepening of awareness: the Latin American theology of liberation, the gruesome struggle for liberation taking place especially in Central America, and the refreshing emergence of the Basic Ecclesial Communities (*Comunidades Eclesiais de Base*—CEBs).

Fr. Alvaro Barreiro, S.J., professor of systematic theology at the Pontifical Catholic University of Rio de Janeiro and pastor of a poor parish in the outskirts of that city, provides us with a theological interpretation of the Basic Ecclesial Community as it has developed in Brazil. He combines solid scriptural and theological resources with first-hand knowledge of these communities themselves. While the CEBs are frequently mentioned particularly in pastoral circles in the United States, there is almost a complete lack of solid information in English on the subject.

At the very outset of his study Fr. Barreiro points to something that seems to have been forgotten if, indeed, it ever sank in: the preferential option for the poor, which the Latin American bishops in solemn assembly in Puebla in 1978 affirmed as the Church's first priority for their local churches, is not merely a regional orientation or one that flows peculiarly from the virulent forms of injustice found in Latin America. The option for the poor is simply an exigency of divine revelation, of Sacred Scripture itself, and of the Church's millennial tradition. In a word, the option for the poor is at the heart of the gospel. For that very reason this option is at the heart of every authentic form of renewal in the Church anywhere and at any time.

The birth of the Basic Ecclesial Communities is a startling example of what can happen when the Church takes seriously the Lord's command to preach the good news to the poor. As Fr. Barreiro points out in his study, the CEBs are the gift of the Spirit, and of the poor who constitute them, to the faithful of Latin America and beyond.

In developed countries such as the United States renewal has so often meant reform of outward modes of ecclesial life such as the liturgy and the organizational models of the parish. Reform has not always meant something more profound and, of course, challenging: special outreach to the poor, a sharpening of interest in and a corresponding commitment to questions of social justice and the creation of a new image for the Church as a Church of the poor, the downtrodden, and the forgotten. The concept of Christian conversion—so essential to any kind of real renewal—has remained a matter of individual spirituality or, even worse, piety dichotomized from the nitty-gritty of the social question. Yet it is conversion to the other, especially to the poor, that verifies the conversion to the Other who is God. Our Latin American neighbors are surely providing us with an extraordinary example of renewal and Christian conversion in these more authentic senses.

It is to be hoped that this example will promote practical pastoral experiments among and with marginalized Christians within North American society. There are painful signs that the situation of socio-economic deprivation and political powerlessness are not the case only in Latin America. In our own country blacks, Hispanics, poor whites in Appalachia, undocumented workers, and the elderly share many of the same plights with their Latin American brothers and sisters. These realities are "the signs of the times" upon which the United States Catholic Church and all committed Christians must base their policies and pastoral activities. These realities also suggest that a new stage in the history of the North American Catholic Church is in the making. They point to the gradual transformation of that Church from one that in this century won national acceptance and even respectability to one that now, in these very different and emerging circumstances, dares to challenge the national and international structures of injustice, selfishness, and complacency of which our nation is undeniably a part.

Since Fr. Barreiro's book first appeared there have been encouraging developments in the Basic Ecclesial Communities in Brazil. They have continued to grow in virtually every part of the country, doubling their numbers to approximately 80,000 in 1981 compared to the 40,000 when Fr. Barreiro wrote his book four years before. Two more Inter-Ecclesial Meetings took place: the Third in João Pessoa (Paraíba) in July 1978 and the Fourth in Itaicí (São Paulo) in April 1981. In each case the numbers of participants grew and became more representative of the Church in almost every part of this immense nation. The fourth meeting gathered representatives from seventy dioceses and, as has always been the case, was encouraged by the enthusiastic support of the leadership of the National Conference of Brazilian Bishops.

Another striking development in the reality of the CEBs in Brazil is the political awareness and weight they represent at this particularly crucial phase of Brazilian history when the political arrangement imposed upon the country by the military and the multinational elites is showing more and more signs of exhaustion. The theme of the Fourth Inter-Ecclesial Meeting was "An Oppressed People Organize Themselves for Liberation." The representatives of the CEBs—small farmers, factory workers, migrants, housewives, and representatives of Brazil's indigenous peoples—wrestled with the relationship between their communities and civil society, partisan politics and political struggle in general. (An outline of their carefully wrought conclusions is available in the *Revista Eclesiástica Brasileira* for July 1981.)

The sense of democratic participation, mutual responsibility, and political awareness characteristic of the thousands of CEBs in Brazil represents a development of historic dimensions for that country. For the first time in Brazilian history the popular classes have found a truly participatory and democratic form of organization *at the national level*. Thus there are those who believe that the CEBs have become the single most important aspect of the evolution of a less authoritarian and more participatory society in general. The CEBs surely are providing a real experience of participation, a sense of what it means to become a subject in one's own history, that rarely has been possible in Brazil's colonial and neocolonial past.

One other development that certainly deserves mention is the official recognition and approval given the Basic Ecclesial Communities by the Latin American bishops at the Puebla Conference in 1979. That Conference clearly established the CEBs as a particularly relevant form of evangelization that is here to stay.

Given these truly hopeful developments, the appearance in English of Fr. Barreiro's book is very timely. North American Christian communities need to be informed about the good news coming out of Latin America.

In a way that reveals a basic involvement with grassroot pastoral realities and excellent sources for theological reflection, Fr. Barreiro spells out the ultimate meaning and value at stake in the evangelization of the poor as this process has unfolded in Latin America: in this process the Church discovers its fullest identity, in it the Church discovers the Lord.

ALLAN FIGUEROA DECK, S.J.
Director of Hispanic Ministry
Diocese of Orange in California

ABBREVIATIONS

CEB	*Comunidades Eclesiais de Base* (Basic Ecclesial Communities)
CNBB	*Conferência Nacional dos Bispos do Brasil* (National Conference of Brazilian Bishops)
EN	*Evangelii Nuntiandi,* apostolic exhortation of Paul VI, December 8, 1975
GS	*Gaudium et Spes,* Constitution on the Church in the Modern World, Vatican II
LG	*Lumen Gentium,* Dogmatic Constitution on the Church, Vatican II
SEDOC	*Serviço de Documentaçao* (Documentation Service), Petrópolis, Brazil

INTRODUCTION

There are times and circumstances in the history of the Church when the gospel is heard and accepted as the good news of the Kingdom, in its original newness. On such occasions, the gospel demonstrates its force for liberation and salvation, giving sight to blind eyes, opening deaf ears, untying mute tongues, and stirring and converting consciences and hearts. All this occurs when "the poor hear the good news" (Luke 7:22). When the good news is preached to the poor, in a pure, free, and fearless manner, it kindles in them the fire of hope, transforming their lives. This is what is happening in thousands of Basic Ecclesial Communities (*Comunidades Eclesiais de Base*—CEBs) scattered throughout all of Brazil. By insertion into the concrete reality of their lives, the gospel is prompting those communities to create new forms of life and, in a joint endeavor, to invent new types of open, committed, and fraternal communities.

The CEBs are, in fact, becoming places, focal points, and vehicles for evangelization, as has already been observed by the Medellín Conference.[1] In them, there is being accomplished what Paul VI, in his apostolic exhortation "Evangelii Nuntiandi" (EN), of December 8, 1975, claimed to be "their most fundamental vocation": "as hearers of the gospel which is proclaimed to them and privileged beneficiaries of evangelization," they will soon become proclaimers of the gospel themselves" (EN 58). This is not just another option, nor a mere imperative. It is already a reality. We are convinced that the CEBs in Brazil today are places for and focal points of evangelization, because the vast majority of them are communities of the poor. In them and through them "the poor are hearing the good news." We consider this fact to be charged with theological significance, and destined to carry deci-

1

sive weight when it is time to select priorities concerning the recipients and the means of evangelization.

In this study, we intend to reflect upon that fact theologically. The study is not complete, even with regard to the subject mentioned in the title. The data on which the theological reflection is based were taken almost exclusively from twenty-nine reports sent to the First and Second Inter-Ecclesial Meetings of the Basic Ecclesial Communities, held in Vitória from January 6 to 8, 1975, and from July 29 to August 1, 1976, respectively, which were published in Nos. 81, 95, and 96 of SEDOC (Documentation Service). It is extremely abundant material, but still very limited when we consider the fact that the number of CEBs in Brazil is estimated at 40,000.

The study is arranged as follows. After a first part containing a brief recollection of how the matter of the relationship between the mystery of the poor, the mystery of Christ, and the mystery of the Church was viewed at Vatican Council II (Chapter I), an attempt is made to show, with data taken from the reports of the communities themselves, the state of poverty and even misery among the Christians who are their members (Chapter II). It will be noted that the members of the CEBs studied in this work, both within and on the outskirts of urban areas, are living under extreme conditions of deprivation and socio-economic neglect. It is important to dwell at length on the explanation of these data, in order to arrive subsequently at a better understanding, by way of contrast, of the liberating force of the gospel which those poor, marginated people accept and experience in their lives. In the third part (Chapter III), after a brief analysis of the biblical terminology relating to the poor, a theological interpretation is made of the status of those same poor people from the Old Testament, especially in the Prophets and Psalms; and, finally, there is an explanation of the biblical grounds for the "privilege of the poor." In the central part of the study (Chapter IV), consecutive comparisons are made of the Gospel according to Luke, Matthew, and Paul, with the living evangelical experiences of the CEBs. The fifth part (Chapter V) is an attempt to answer the question of how the good news of liberation proclaimed to the poor by Jesus is fulfilled in the CEBs. After the problem is posed in all its seriousness and a preliminary question is answered, the mission of the

Church to carry the good news to the poor, continuing Jesus' mission, is set forth and substantiated. Next, there is a description of the "signs" which show how the good news of the coming of the Kingdom announced by Jesus to the poor is fulfilled, concretely, in the CEBs. In the final part (Chapter VI), two questions that may be regarded as conclusions of the study as a whole are selected. The subject of the evangelization of the poor in the CEBs is now viewed, no longer from a predominantly objective standpoint: the poor who are evangelized; but rather from a subjective standpoint: the poor who evangelize. The two questions are (1) Can the poor be the evangelizers and liberators of their oppressors? (2) How can the poor in the CEBs evangelize and liberate the very Church from which they received the gospel of liberation?

The CEBs came into existence, and are still doing so, in Brazil, with the spontaneity and multiformity that are typical of the action of the Spirit and of the diversity of the local conditions. But there is a common element comprising all of them: the interpretation of the concrete life of the communities in the light of the Word of God. Any theology which intends to be Christian theology must be ecclesial; it must be carried out within the community, and based upon the faith of the community. Hence, a theological reflection on the experiences of the CEBs in Brazil is in its "natural place" at the outset. Essentially, the method used in our study is the same one used by the CEBs: an interpretation of the facts (in this instance, regarding the concrete Christian existence of those communities) in the light of the Word of God and the living faith of the Church.

The poor Christians who comprise the CEBs are unfamiliar with any of the forms of triumphalism. They do not even have a reflective awareness of the evangelical treasures of which they are the bearers. The idea of appearing as "models" would never occur to them. They are simply striving to "do the truth." And it is an indisputable fact that the truth of the gospel is transforming their lives and those of their communities and is converting and liberating them. If we allow ourselves to be challenged by the witness of Christian life in those communities of the poor, we too shall progress a little farther along the path of conversion, truth, and liberty of the gospel of Jesus Christ.

I

VATICAN COUNCIL II, EVANGELIZATION OF THE POOR, AND CEBs

On the occasion of Vatican Council II, there was considerable reflection, discussion, and writing on the subject of the Church and poverty, the Church of the poor, the evangelization of the poor, and the mystery of the poor and its relationship to the mystery of Christ and the Church.[1] Two addresses served as a catalyst for the aspirations and reflection of the Council Fathers on this topic: Pope John XXIII's radio message exactly one month before the opening of the Council, and Cardinal Lercaro's address in the Council Hall at the end of the first session.

In his message of September 11, John XXIII declared: "With respect to the underdeveloped countries, the Church appears as it is and wants to be: the Church of all people and, in particular, the Church of the poor."[2] When taken literally, this comment is more accurate as a *de jure* affirmation than as a *de facto* confirmation.[3] Concerning the present Church, considered sociologically and as a whole, one would have to say, changing John XXIII's assertion, that it is the Church of everyone, but especially the rich.[4] The Pope's assertion is truer as an optative and imperative (what the Church intends and ought to be) than as an indicative (what it is). His remarks were, in fact, interpreted in this way, and had remarkable repercussions not only within but also outside of the

4

Council. Commenting on the Pope's statement, G. Hourdin wrote: "During the past two centuries, the Church of Christ has appeared to many as being reserved for a few tens of millions of rich and white people." Since the industrial and scientific revolution occurred, "the majority of the faithful in the Church have been rich members of the middle and upper classes or conservative rural people of the white race, who have protected their temporal interests by invoking the Church's name." Hourdin concludes by stating: "What we want from the Fathers meeting in the Council is that they say in clear-cut terms what John XXIII has said; that they will make incumbent upon everyone the obligation to share their goods and to assume a place, collectively, on the side of those who are hungry and thirsty. . . . We want this from them, and nothing else, because nothing else is of equal importance."[5] René Laurentin expressed the same view: "To many bishops, one of the Council's greatest problems lies in the matter of the Church's becoming, on a grand scale, the Church of the poor."[6]

Yves Congar has written: "While the entire mystique of the Church affirms love for the poor, and even for poverty, and while the Church is really poor almost everywhere, and at times even indigent, it *appears* to be rich and, to tell the truth, lordly, or seeking to be such. In this way, it has caused itself harm, and it has harmed the cause which it exists to serve and which it is really intended to serve."[7] This is a truly intolerable situation for a conscience with Christian insight and sentiment, to which a practical response must be given. Another contrasting aspect of this same essential problem has been explained by M. D. Chenu as follows: "On the one hand, it is undeniable that, throughout the course of its history, the Church has always been the resort of the weak, the deprived, the voiceless, the poor; it has undertaken the social services that governments could not or would not perform—educating children, caring for the sick, sheltering the aged, and, more recently, helping the handicapped—functions which, even in the industrial civilization of today, it still carries out in certain underdeveloped areas. But on the other hand there is much truth in the prevailing opinion that the poor receive little credit or support in the Church; there, as in society at large, they find themselves marginalized."[8]

But, let us leave the commentators and return to the Council.

Cardinal Lercaro, in his famous address of December 6, 1962,[9] criticized the schemas on the Church for not offering, in the doctrine on the Church itself, the essential, primary revelation of the mystery of Christ, namely, his presence among the poor. The cardinal from Bologna argued that the Council could not shed light on the mystery of the Church, the "sacrament of Christ," without bringing up "the mystery of Christ among the poor." Consequently, he requested that priority be given to the "preparation of the evangelical doctrine on the preeminent dignity of the poor as privileged members of the Church"; that "the center and spirit of all the doctrinal and legislative work [of the Council] be the mystery of Christ among the poor and the evangelization of the poor"; and that, "in the improvement of the schemas on the adaptation of the institutions and the methods of evangelization, account always be taken of the historical relationship that exists between recognition of the preeminent dignity of the poor and the effective reform of the Church."

The evangelization of the poor did not become the "theme" of the Council, as Cardinal Lercaro requested in his address.[10] Although there are many scattered references to the matter of the poor, particularly in the two major conciliar constitutions, *Lumen Gentium* (sixteen times) and *Gaudium et Spes* (fourteen times), from a quantitative standpoint it occupies a minor position. In LG 8, however, there is a statement with the same Christological viewpoint vigorously adopted by Cardinal Lercaro,[11] on the essential role played by the revelation about poverty.[12]

The appearance and expansion of the CEBs in Brazil are contemporaneous with Vatican Council II. Several reports expressly cite the Council as one of the determining factors in the creation of the CEBs. On a purely historical basis, no appropriate causal relationship between the two events can be proven. What both have in common is the action of the same Spirit who, through charisms, works (at times overcoming obstacles that are unsurmountable for human efforts) among the holders of the episcopal ministry, gathered in a conciliar assembly, to enable them to carry out that ministry according to the needs of the times. And the Spirit also works among the faithful in the CEBs, leading them to discern and fully understand, in their state of abandonment and alienation, "signs" of the presence and action of God's salvific plan in history (see GS 11). Because the Spirit of the Lord is liberty (2 Cor. 3:17) and blows where it wills (John 3:8), the Council did not suspect, nor could it have suspected, that the issue of the evangelization of the poor would become a reality, in such a "poor" and such an "evangelical" manner, in the CEBs. Among the poor people of the CEBs in Brazil, there is actually rising up and growing, through the power of the Spirit, a Church of the poor which, leading a life of evangelical service, is questioning, without attempting to do so directly, life styles that are in contradiction to the gospel, both within and outside of the Church.

II

THE CEBs, COMMUNITIES
OF THE POOR

Nearly all the CEBs in Brazil, located in the rural areas and, to a lesser extent, in the poor neighborhoods on the outskirts of cities, are communities of the poor.[1] According to the study prepared by IBRADES (Brazilian Development Institute) from a hundred reports sent from the various regional bodies of the CNBB (National Conference of Brazilian Bishops), the locations of the CEBs, according to area, are as follows: 53.5 percent in the rural area, 10.9 percent in the suburban area, and 16.8 percent in the urban area.[2] All the communities which are mentioned in the twenty-nine reports sent to the First and Second Inter-Ecclesial Meetings of the Basic Ecclesial Communities, held in Vitória, are also located in the rural area or on the outskirts of cities.[3] This information, combined with other data that might be analyzed, shows that the social context has decisively determined the formation of the CEBs.[4] But what is of concern to us, in the context of our study, is to reflect theologically on the fact that the vast majority of the CEBs in Brazil are comprised of poor people. However, the anonymous figures in the statistics conceal the lives and histories of the concrete individuals and communities. Hence, we shall enlarge upon some of the information from the aforementioned reports sent to the meetings in Vitória which shows us, in a more existential manner, how those poor people who make up nearly all of the CEBs live.[5]

8

In Tacaimbo, a town of 3,000 inhabitants located 165 kilometers from Recife, everything is lacking: employment, housing, food, health, and schools. "The vast majority of the people lead lives of doing without," oppressed, and afflicted by the vicious circle of poverty which, with cumulative causes, spreads like a cancer. It is the members of the CEBs who describe themselves as follows: "The poor majority have no fixed work; they work for hire in the fields, earning 12 cruzeiros a day [in April 1976 one dollar was worth 10.35 cruzeiros]. That fieldwork does not provide enough to live, but only to vegetate. This is why many experience hunger. The people . . . thank God when they have beans, corn, and manioc root meal. Such *'food'* does not provide enough to live. They live by moral force; they live because they withstand it somehow. There is meat for one day, but for eight days there is none. Health is very poor. Sometimes a father has five or six children, and four die. They die of need, disregarded, because they cannot be treated. Hence, most of the diseases occur among the children. Many adults are also sick, and cannot buy medicine. There are sick people in almost all the houses. Most of the people here in Tacaimbo reside in flimsy dwellings, in mud huts. There is almost no sanitation in those dwellings, they have no cesspools. All the children have swollen bellies, and are vomiting with dysentery, which is endless. The school facilities are very unstable. What is learned from them is rubbish. I have a daughter who has been in school for three years, and she is just now learning how to write her name."[6]

The state of neglect, deprivation, and extreme poverty is similar in the parish of the Immaculate Conception in Barreirinhas. It contains forty-eight CEBs, four in the center and forty-four in the countryside. The territorial area of the parish coincides with that of the municipality of Barreirinhas: 2,347 square kilometers. It has a population of 25,000, 5,000 of whom reside in the center. The roads connecting the communities with one another are few in number and impassable during the rainy season, which lasts for seven months. The Christians who make up these rural communities are "deprived of all resources: cultural, social, economic, and political." Their misery, according to the author of the report, is "perhaps the most deep-seated in Brazil." "Twenty years ago, the farmers were still living without worrying about their survival.

There were always animals in the forest to hunt, and fish in the river. Today, without food supplies, they can easily starve. The woods are becoming depleted, and the soil is impoverished." "They are populations doomed to chronic hunger, established on exhausted land, and also surrounded by large landowners whose infernal circle is increasingly closing in on them."[7]

Other rural CEBs are also poor, although not in such a tragic way. The socio-economic status of the Prelature of Acre and Purus, covering 102,136 square kilometers and containing 200,000 inhabitants, has been described by its bishop, Dom Moacyr, thus: "The lack of industries, the unemployment, the illiteracy, the mass-scale disease, the lack of skilled labor and the low wages, the absence of roads, the outmoded techniques in agriculture, the elimination of the rubber plantations, the conversion of various areas into livestock-raising zones, the arrival of big investors, and many other problems indicate a rather complex reality."[8] In the Maranhão region, bounded by the five municipalities of Santa Rita, Itapecuru, Vargem Grande, Presidente Juscelino, and Morros, there are twenty-two communities, situated in small settlements "connected with one another only by backwoods roads which the residents traverse on foot or horseback. In 1963, there was no medical care or schools in the region, and there were two business firms which served as suppliers and purchasers of products."[9] The people make their living from subsistence farming: rice, beans, corn, babassu palm and, especially, manioc. The soil is tilled without mechanization or animal traction; and yet nearly all the fruits of the labor that are produced under these conditions are taken from the manual laborer: In 1974, the farmer earned 3.71 cruzeiros per *alqueire* [a surface measure varying according to locality] of manioc; whereas the middleman earned 25 cruzeiros.[10] (In June 1974 one dollar was worth 6.89 cruzeiros.)

The small local church in Marroás is situated in the district of the same name, and has a total of 8,000 baptized members, 500 of whom are in the center, and the rest in 52 settlements. The report describes the economy of the region as follows: "It raises cattle, sheep, and goats; the agriculture includes cotton, corn, beans, castor beans, manioc, bananas, and papaya. There is some commercial activity in the center, and there are two streets passable by vehicles, but they are far from the central area. There are five large landowners, several small ones, and many landless farmers."[11] The "account" prepared by a few members of the evangelization group of the Sítio Granjeiro community, in the parish of Mogeiro begins as follows: "The status of the area occupied by us consists of a lack of land and of grass planted for oxen, causing an exodus to the south; there is disease, a lack of mutual cooperation, death of children, and hunger (misery)."[12]

The parish of São Mateus, with 20,000 inhabitants, approximately 5,000 of whom reside in the center, is "essentially rural, with a large amount of immigration from Ceara and Piaui."[13] When the experiment of creating the CEBs began in 1973, the "church was attended by a small group, nearly all humble people."[14] The amount of the tithe, which was established for the purpose of achieving self-support for the parish, was one cruzeiro per month. (In June 1973 one dollar was worth 6.10 cruzieros.) The same state of extreme poverty is disclosed by this information from the community of Olho d'Aguinha dos Freires, in the parish of Poranga: "For the small pharmacy, we hold a fraternal fund raiser among the forty-five families in the community. From the receipts, we purchase the most necessary medicines. We resell the medicine to the people, so as always to have money to buy medicines when the supply is depleted."[15] In the same community there is "a group of thirty-five who made a funding plan, with a loan of 200 cruzeiros, to be paid in two years."[16]

The experience of the CEBs in the rural area of the diocese of São Mateus "applies mainly to the class that is most underprivileged from a social standpoint. The more wealthy (in money and culture) almost never show up."[17] The community of Espírito Santo, one of seventy in the parish of São Mateus, consists of forty black families, twenty of whom have assumed responsibility for the community.[18] The report from Goias states: "The vast majority of our 'baptized' people, who are hence official members of the Church, are the poor and oppressed. The system becomes more burdensome for them every day, increasing the poverty and exacerbating the oppression."[19]

There are thirty-three CEBs scattered among the rural parishes of São Domingos and Novo Brasil. Their members are farmers, mostly sharecroppers, and at best, small landowners.[20] The parish of Our Lady of Christian Help in Itarana has 20,000 inhabitants, covers 900 square kilometers and includes twenty chapels. The parishioners are almost exclusively colonists of German and Italian origin, and the majority are poor and illiterate. They live on subsistence crops, particularly corn. The means of production are extremely primitive, the terrain is rough, and there is exploitative marketing of products. Roads passable by vehicles exist only between the far points of the larger towns. It is a region without a future, and therefore eroded by vast emigration of the youth to the centers with greater opportunities.[21]

The forty communities scattered throughout the interior of the municipality of Linhares, with 110,000 inhabitants, 40,000 of whom reside in the interior, are rural as well. In the communities, there are five distinctive ethnic groups, with the following features. The Indian group (four communities): nearly all the adults are illiterate; very listless and prone to alcoholism; they make their living from fishing and farming, growing manioc in particular. The African group (eight communities): also nearly all illiterate; rather listless, working only enough to avoid dying, as manual laborers in clearing cocoa fields, making charcoal, and working on cattle ranches; they are fatalists, and very much given to alcoholism. The Italian group (nine communities): landowners in good economic circumstances; 70 percent of the adults are illiterate. The German group (six communities): they are very industrious and prosperous; there are many internal rivalries and much alcoholism; illiterates are rare. The mixed group: they share the qualities and shortcomings of the aforementioned groups; 70 percent are manual laborers, employed in sawmills, planting cocoa, and making charcoal; they live on a minimum wage, and do not earn even that when they work at planting cocoa; the families are very large, with an average of seven or eight children per family, because "it is God who gives the children."[22]

The CEBs located on the outskirts of the cities are also poor, and at times very poor. For example, all the communities on the outskirts of Vitória are communities of the poor, most of whom are laborers from the interior of Minas and Espírito Santo, who are unemployed or underemployed, or are municipal employees. Those CEBs are situated in newly formed districts and in slums built over mangrove swamps or on hillsides.[23] The parish of São

Sebastião in Alto de Pasqual, located in the Recife suburban belt, has about 50,000 inhabitants. Submerged in this expanse which extends over "heights" and "ravines," from 150 to 200 people are trying to live in a community with "diaspora status." Catholicism has disappeared as a predominant and "visible" religion; the Church makes no impression, with either its size or its wealth. The evangelical acceptance of a Church that is a "minority," a "seed," with "diaspora status," has proven very difficult for them.[24] In the Rangel district of João Pessoa, there are twenty-five communities of adults, eight youth groups, and fifteen children's groups. They are very poor families living in hovels built without any sanitary facilities. There is a high incidence of schistosomiasis and tuberculosis. "The district's population consists of about 28,000 inhabitants originating in towns of the interior and the Jaguaribe district which, as they became middle class, caused the families with low or no income to leave for Rangel."[25] "The people's occupations are as follows: small merchants, minor public, state, and municipal employees, members of the military, teachers, drivers, nursing aides, domestics, seamstresses, laundresses, laborers (service personnel, bricklayers, electricians, plumbers, watchmen, and mechanics) doing odd jobs and underemployed. The number of unemployed and beggars is large."[26] The environment of the CEBs in Volta Redonda is an "environment of laborers and poor people." The work of the CEBs is "quite acceptable in the more unassuming environment, and even where there is economic poverty." But it is not accepted in middle-class environments, much less among the well-to-do.[27]

The fact that virtually all the CEBs in Brazil are communities of the poor has been confirmed by the observations made at the General Assembly of Bishops of São Paulo, the wealthiest state in the nation. The summary of the reports from the twenty-nine dioceses states, among other things: "The creation of the CEBs has taken place among the lower socio-economic classes. And, in the poor areas, it has been noted that the most underprivileged have been the ones most receptive to this ecclesial notion. The difficulties among the other classes are considerable, and when ecclesial groups come into existence, they often become closed, and introspective."[28]

III

THE POOR
IN THE OLD TESTAMENT

The Poor in Biblical Terminology[1]

The concrete vocabulary of the Hebrew language evokes the procession of the poor bearing their misfortunes: together with *rash,* the "pauper," there is *dal,* the "lean" or "weak," *ebion,* the unsatisfied "beggar," *ani* (the term most often used in the Old Testament: eighty times, particularly by the Prophets and in the Psalms), and *anaw,* the "bowed and broken" person.[2]

To us Westerners, the poor person is, first of all, one who has few economic goods and who, consequently, suffers deprivation. The Semite is particularly sensitive to the social inferiority of the poor person: the poor person is the defenseless human being, who has no opportunity to assert his or her rights to the justice system, because it is in the hands of the unjust, the violent, the powerful. Therefore that person is a victim of humiliation, abuse, and all kinds of injustice. Etymologically, the *anawim* are the "humiliated, the downtrodden, and the abased." "Their misery, which makes them incapable of asserting themselves, places them in heavy dependence on others; they are forced to 'humble themselves,' and they have no means of defending themselves or resisting."[3]

Although the Old Testament focuses directly and primarily on the social alienation of the poor, at the same time it quite clearly

14

detects the economic and political roots of that alienation. The root cause of the impotence of the poor person to assert his or her rights is that person's indigence. Because the poor do not have the material means for subsistence, they cannot assert themselves in relation to others, owing to the lack of either voice or opportunity. Because the poor are indigent, they are frequently ill and unemployed; if the poor want to continue living, they must accept jobs in which they are exploited and oppressed by those who hold the economic and political power.[4]

The language of the Gospels reveals this very essential concept:[5] it does not mention poverty directly, but speaks rather of the poor. The usual term for describing the state of poverty is *ptochos* (Gr., one who cringes), which appears twenty-four times: five in Matthew, five in Mark, ten in Luke, and four in John. The poor are by no means idealized. In three quarters of the cases (eighteen out of twenty-four), they are indigent persons, needing material assistance, who must be helped.[6] In biblical terminology, those who have no place to live, nothing to wear, and nothing to eat belong to the poor class:[7] the blind, the deaf, the crippled; the prisoners, the strangers, the orphans, and the widows; the afflicted, the depressed, and the hopeless. To summarize, the biblical concept of the poor includes all categories of unfortunate, neglected people who are suffering and weeping because of their social inferiority; the feeble, weak members of society, who feel and who really are defenseless, helpless, and unprotected; those who have neither a voice nor an opportunity in society.

Theological Interpretation of the Status of the Poor in the Old Testament

The fact that the concept of the poor as we have just described it is not found in the more ancient sources of the Old Testament is significant. The description of the oppressed poor appears increasingly frequent after the nomadic tribal federation gave way to a kingdom. The new and increasing socio-economic imbalances were viewed by the authors of the Bible as a flagrant contradiction of the Covenant, and hence as an injustice and a sin.

Israel made a theological interpretation of the dialectics between the oppressed and the oppressor in the light of its faith in

defender of the poor, but not poverty

the God of the Covenant. The powerful one who oppresses the poor is an "irreligious" person who does not fear God. But God is the defender of the rights of the poor. This idea that God is the defender of the poor, and of all the neglected and oppressed, is one of the great *Leitmotiven* pervading the entire Old Testament, and appearing most directly and vehemently in the Prophets and the wisdom literature, owing to the new socio-economic situations.[8]

Throughout the Psalms, (the religious expression of the Israelite's spirituality), for example, there is a long procession of Israel's "wretched of the earth": the indigent and sick, the calumniated, those (unjustly!) accused and persecuted, the refugees and those in exile. The appeals for help of all those poor people, the cry of all those unfortunate ones rises from the depths of their anguish and oppression to God, filled with unbounded hope in the fidelity of the Lord, who will liberate them, making divine justice triumph over the oppressors. This is how that hope and faith are expressed in Psalm 9:

> So may the Lord be a tower of strength for the oppressed,
> a tower of strength in time of need,
> that those who acknowledge thy name may trust in thee;
> for thou, Lord, dost not forsake those who seek thee. . . .
> For the Avenger of blood has remembered man's desire,
> and has not forgotten the cry of the poor. . . .
> But the poor shall not always be unheeded,
> nor the hope of the destitute be always in vain
>   [Ps. 9–10, 12, 18].[9]

At times, the cry for help addressed to God, the "refuge for the oppressed," ends on a note of confidence in God, who eventually overcomes the terror caused by the irreligious. We have an example in Psalm 10:

> The wicked man in his pride hunts down the poor. . . .
> Arrogant as he is, he scorns the Lord
> and leaves no place for God in all his schemes. . . .
> His mouth is full of lies and violence;
> mischief and trouble lurk under his tongue
>   [Ps. 10: 2, 4, 7].

In verses 8–10, the psalmist describes how the irreligious person spies upon the innocent, so as to kill them by stealth, like a trap catching the poor, and like a lion crouching to seize its victim.[10] And he concludes with an expression of devotion to and confidence in the Lord:

> The poor victim commits himself to thee;
> fatherless, he finds in thee a helper. . . .
> Thou hast heard the lament of the humble, O Lord,
> and art attentive to their heart's desire,
> bringing justice to the orphan and the downtrodden
> that fear may never drive men from their homes again
> [Ps. 10: 14b, 17].

The absolute certainty of God's intervention to put an end to the violence visited upon the poor is expressed in these verses from Psalm 12:

> "For the ruin of the poor, for the groans of the needy,
> now I will arise," says the Lord,
> "I will place him in the safety for which he longs."
> Do thou, Lord, protect us
> and guard us from a profligate and evil generation
> [Ps. 12: 5, 7].

We shall now offer, as we have done with the Psalms, a selection of texts in which the Prophets appear as fearless defenders of all the poor, oppressed, and defenseless, in the name of God. The biblical prophets are, essentially, God's ambassadors who, in a mystical experience, receive from God the mission of announcing the demands of the Covenant to the king, the priests, and the people of their time. Paradoxically, the Prophets were "revolutionaries," because they were intransigently conservative in the literal sense of the term: adamantly faithful to the ancient rule of the Covenant, based on justice and right.[11]

The texts selected here are well known; but, when reread from the standpoint of the status of the poor in the CEBs, they assume a new timeliness, and a new force for conversion. In their time (the second quarter of the eighth century B.C.), the commercial exchanges with foreigners were increasing the socio-economic imbalances between the rich and the poor. In other words, there was an increase in the exploitation of the needy by the powerful. The prophet Amos, whose ministry lasted only a few months, [12] denounced the crimes committed among the people of the Covenant: the greed for wealth, the commercial fraudulence, the venality and corruption of judges, the ostentation of the rich, and the oppression of the poor.

> Because they sell the innocent for silver
> and the destitute for a pair of shoes.
> They grind the heads of the poor into the earth
> and thrust the humble out of their way [Amos 2:6b, 7a].

> You that turn justice upside down [13]
> and bring righteousness to the ground . . .
> because you levy taxes on the poor
> and extort a tribute of grain from them. . . .
> You who persecute the guiltless,
> hold men to ransom
> and thrust the destitute out of court [Amos 5:7, 11, 12b].

> Listen to this, you who grind the destitute and plunder the
>   humble [Amos 8:4].

The same themes are reiterated by the first Isaiah:

> Shame on you! you who make unjust laws
> and publish burdensome decrees,
> depriving the poor of justice,
> robbing the weakest of my people of their rights,
> despoiling the widow and plundering the orphan.
> What will you do when called to account,
> when ruin from afar confronts you? [Isa. 10:1–3].

The prophet Micah was a contemporary of Isaiah. He observed a worsening of the social situation, with a widening of the gap between rich and poor. With the courage that he acquired from the call of the Lord, he announced the judgment of God, who will not tolerate injustice. Micah fought alone before the people, whose suffering he shared, and before the powerful, whose venality he denounced. Both his announcement and his denunciation are an appeal for conversion. Addressing the leaders of Israel, he called them violent and voracious, "haters of good and lovers of evil," who "flay people," "devouring their flesh," and "splintering their bones." "Then they will call to the Lord, and he will give them no answer . . . so wicked are their deeds" (see Mic. 3:1–4).

The prophet Jeremiah, born in the middle of the seventh century B.C., lived during the most dramatic period of Israel's history: that of the preparation for the ruin of Judah, the exiles, and the destruction of the city and the temple of Jerusalem in 587. He had to battle against everyone: the kings, priests, false prophets, people, and even the members of his own family. His fidelity to the prophetic ministry made him not only a solitary person, but also an alienated one, in the literal sense of the word. Accused of defeatism, persecuted, and imprisoned, he was finally forced to go to Egypt, where he probably died. Following are some examples of his prophetic remarks against the people and, especially, the kings of Judah, wherein he denounces the injustices and violence committed upon the poor.

> There is blood on the corners of your robe—
> the life-blood of the innocent poor.
> You did not get it by housebreaking [2:34].

> For among my people there are wicked men . . .
> Their houses are full of fraud,
> as a cage is full of birds.
> They grow rich and grand,
> bloated and rancorous;
> their thoughts are all of evil
> and they refuse to do justice,
> the claims of the orphan they do not put right
> nor do they grant justice to the poor [5:26–28].

The same demands are expressed positively in the prophecies addressed to the kings of Judah:

> Administer justice betimes,
> rescue the victim from his oppressor,

lest the fire of my fury blaze up and burn unquenched
because of your evil doings [21:12].

These are the words of the Lord: Deal justly and fairly, res-
cue the victim from his oppressor, do not ill-treat or do
violence to the alien, the orphan, or the widow, do not shed
innocent blood in this place [22:3].

The prophet Jeremiah contrasts the tryannical behavior of
King Johoiakim, the puppet-vassal who ordered the construction
of a new palace using slave labor,[14] with the conduct of King Jo-
siah, who

dealt justly and fairly. . . .
He dispensed justice to the lowly and poor;
did not this show he knew me? says the Lord.
But you have no eyes,
no thought for anything but gain,
set only on the innocent blood you can shed
on cruel acts of tyranny [22:15–17].

Israel's view of the poor gradually assumes a moral and religious tone. The "cry of the poor" reverberating throughout the
Book of Psalms is not only the cry of the indigent, but also that of
all the afflicted. After the exile, poor (*ani*) becomes a synonym
for religious. However, these poor people are always economically poor, or needy (persecuted) in some way, as well.[15] The poor,
whom God loves with merciful and benevolent love, are the humble (*anawim*) who "bow" before God, God's power, and God's
plan of salvation; those who seek God, who walk in God's sight,
and who trust in God, even in their ordeals.[16]

Biblical Grounds for the "Privilege of the Poor"

As we shall observe subsequently, all these poor people will be
proclaimed as blessed by Jesus; they will be the privileged recipients of the Kingdom of God. What is the reason, what are the
grounds for this "privilege of the poor"?

The entire Old Testament (the Law, and particularly the
Prophets, owing to the new historical situations) at all times as-

sumes a position on behalf of the defenseless and oppressed poor. This point acquires special significance in light of the Old Testament theological viewpoint regarding the king's image. As a substitute for God, the king must make righteousness and justice prevail and is specifically entrusted with the preservation and defense of the rights of the poor, the weak, and the defenseless.[17] This matter has been studied extensively by Jacque Dupont, particularly in his authoritative study on the Beatitudes. "The grounds for what may be termed the privilege of the poor are not to be found in an idealized concept of their poverty, but rather in an ideal of their real function."[18] In other words, they do not lie in the internal spiritual inclinations of the poor, but rather in God, in God's inclination, "in the way in which God conceives of the exercise of the divine kingship on behalf of the weak and unfortunate."[19]

In this respect, the Bible reflects the notion that the entire ancient East had of the ideal kingdom, beginning in the third millennium. In both Mesopotamia and Egypt, the king's main function was to ensure justice for his subjects. In exercising this prerogative, the king had to take into account a de facto situation: among his subjects, along with the powerful and the rich, who would always tend to take advantage of the means at their disposal to exploit and oppress the weak, there were weak human beings, the poor and the abandoned, incapable of defending themselves. They were at the mercy of the powerful. If the king was really worthy of his position, he would, therefore, have to become the defender of the poor, the widows, the orphans, and the oppressed. He would be the accredited protector of the weak, causing their rights to be upheld and eliminating the mistreatment of which they were the victims. From this standpoint, one infers the ideal of a royal justice, one that is not exactly impartial, but which takes the side of the weak against the strong and of the poor against the rich. Under a perfect king, who effectively exercised his prerogative as a defender of justice, the latter would not benefit all the subjects alike: the humble and the little people would be the beneficiaries, while the powerful and the violent would be prevented from harming others.[20]

Israel shared this same general attitude of the ancient East. In Psalm 72 (perhaps a prayer on coronation day), solicitude for all the oppressed appears to be a characteristic and preeminent function of the king. Israel beseeches God that the king, elected by God to defend and govern the people on the basis of truth and justice, may actually exercise Yahweh's justice, which is always a justice on behalf of the poor, the afflicted, the indigent, and the oppressed:

> He shall give judgment for the suffering
> and help those of the people that are needy;
> he shall crush the oppressor. . . .
> May he have pity on the needy and the poor,
> deliver the poor from death;
> may he redeem them from oppression and violence
> and may their blood be precious in his eyes
>   [Ps. 72:4, 13-14].

"The king who is required to administer Yahweh's law in Israel (verse 1) is judged precisely by his intervention on behalf of those most in need of help. Either he is king of the weakest people, or else he is not a genuine king of Israel."[21]

The religious texts of the ancient East apply to the gods this same type of royal justice on behalf of the poor and the oppressed. Israel also considers Yahweh the protector of the poor, by virtue of Yahweh's royal justice. "In Israel it is considered normal for Yahweh, king of its people, to be the accredited protector of all those who are defenseless. By assuming this role, Yahweh is only exercising the first royal prerogative, which consists of ensuring justice for the weak, the little people, and the poor, punishing all those who might attempt to violate their rights. Yahweh is a just king, but also a merciful and compassionate king, qualities that can only reinforce Yahweh's solicitude for the unfortunate and those who are in distress. Justice and mercy combine here to produce the same effect, jointly justifying the privileged status held by the abandoned in the eyes of God."[22] The argument made concerning the king applies, *a fortiori,* to the God of Israel: If God were not the defender of the oppressed, God would not be just nor merciful—in other words, not the God of Israel.

Israel had the painful, disgraceful experience whereby the poor were oppressed among the chosen people, the people of the Covenant, as well. Its religious conscience was tormented by this question: "Why do the wicked prosper and traitors live at ease?" (Jer. 12: 1). Nevertheless, the people of Israel did not lose their faith in Yahweh's exercise of royal justice, but projected it into the future, to the time of the Messiah, when Yahweh's justice and solicitude for the poor would be carried out. "This is the meaning of the promise which reverberates in such a special way in the second half of the Book of Isaiah. When God institutes the Kingdom, it may be said that God 'has comforted his people and has pity on his own in their distress' (Isa. 49: 13). Then God will make divine justice, mercy, and love prevail, redeeming and saving the oppressed, and taking revenge on their oppressors."[23] When the divine Kingdom is actually established, the God of Israel will manifest the divine power in a way which Luke considered already a reality: putting the arrogant of heart and mind to rout, tearing imperial powers from their thrones, lifting the humble high, satisfying the hungry with good things, and sending the rich empty away (See Luke 1:51–53).

IV

THE GOOD NEWS PROCLAIMED TO THE POOR AND THE CEBs

The Gospel According to Luke and the CEBs

Jesus, the Messiah of the Poor

Jesus is identified with the messenger of Isaiah's prophecy announcing the good news of peace, happiness, and salvation of the Kingdom of God.

> How lovely on the mountains are the feet of the herald
> who comes to proclaim prosperity and bring good news,
> the news of deliverance, calling to Zion,
> "Your God is king" [Isa. 52:7].

The time of the promised "consolation" arrived with Jesus. His mission coincides exactly with the proclamation of the establishment of God's Kingdom. This proclamation is good news, particularly and primarily for the poor, the oppressed, and all those who are unfortunate—the privileged beneficiaries of the Kingdom, in which there must be a "manifestation of the justice which God wishes to exercise on behalf of the defenseless. At the same

24

time this Kingdom manifests the justice God wishes to exercise because of his tender mercy toward those who are unfortunate or suffering distress."[1]

In five of the twenty-four texts in the Gospels wherein the term "poor" (*ptochos*) appears, it has this eschatological meaning specifically.[2] The texts, in Luke's account, are as follows:

1. Jesus was anointed and sent "to evangelize the poor" (Luke 4:18). After having read in the synagogue at Nazareth the prophecy from Isaiah 61:1–2, Jesus outlines the program for his ministry on the basis of it.[3] In it, in his person and his mission, there is present, there is "today," God's expected intervention on behalf of the poor, the imprisoned, the blind, all the oppressed, and all those to whom God announces liberation, and the end of their suffering.

2. A sign of the presence of the Kingdom in the person and mission of Jesus is the fact that "the poor are hearing the good news" (Luke 7:22). When questioned directly by the disciples of John the Baptist regarding his person and mission, Jesus replies by revealing himself in words and deeds. The deeds are the signs of the Kingdom: "There and then he cured many sufferers from diseases, plagues, and evil spirits; and on many blind people he bestowed sight" (Luke 7:21).[4] The verbal response given thereafter consists of a series of references to the prophecies of consolation from the Book of Isaiah: "Go and tell John what you have seen and heard: how the blind recover their sight, the lame walk, the lepers are cured, the deaf hear, the dead are raised to life, the poor are hearing the good news" (Luke 7:22). John may thereby have realized that the promises made for the time of the Messiah were being fulfilled in the ministry of Jesus. Among the signs accrediting him as the liberating Messiah, Jesus lists lastly that the good news is preached to the poor. Although it does not have the miraculous quality of the others, this sign gives the impression of being the most specific and the most decisive of all. "Jesus seems to be making it the most typical, distinctive feature of his mission."[5]

3. The first three Beatitudes are addressed to the poor (deprived of all economic and social support), the hungry (deprived of the means of satisfying their hunger), and the afflicted (who show externally the affliction causing their economic and social aliena-

tion). According to Dupont, they comprise a combined unit that is rooted in the very texts of Isaiah underlying the other two passages. The poor to whom the good news is proclaimed are precisely those who are indigent from a social and economic standpoint, as described previously. Echoing the promises in the Book of Isaiah, and most especially the prophecy in 61:1-2, wherein the messenger proclaiming the good news to all the poor is announced, the first three Beatitudes must represent the most ancient core of Jesus' preaching. Identifying himself with that messenger, Jesus proclaims: "How blest are you who are poor; the kingdom of God is yours" (Luke 6:20). God's justice is manifested, putting an end to all that suffering of the poor.[6]

Jesus Announces a Total Liberation, Within and Without

In a spiritualist, moralizing interpretation, which is quite common,[7] the poor are proclaimed to be blessed, not because of their socio-economic status, but because of their internal spiritual inclinations. Dupont, on the other hand, in his authoritative study of the Beatitudes, upholds the proposition that "the privilege of the poor and the unhappy has its true grounds, not in them or the spiritual inclinations that are ascribed to them, but rather in the nature of the Kingdom which is coming, in the inclinations of God, who wants to exercise the divine royal power on behalf of the most abandoned. The Beatitudes are primarily a revelation of the mercy and justice which must typify the Kingdom of God."[8] "Jesus is addressing, not a group of human beings marked by a religious attitude, but rather the poor, despised and wretched, the people who seem to be excluded from salvation."[9] In opposition to a moralizing exegesis, Dupont also argues using the fact that the same texts which speak about the poor mention the hungry, the imprisoned, the blind, the deaf, the lepers, etc. Now it is obviously impossible to spiritualize the status of all those types of unfortunates.

Nevertheless, the privilege of the poor is not exclusive.[10] In Luke's universalist theology, the salvation proclaimed by Jesus is offered to everyone. In the Nazareth programmatic discourse (Luke 4:16-30) which, in its present form, may be a composition of the evangelist, but must hark back to Jesus himself in its historical essence, is proclaimed a total liberation, within and without. "Its message was a religious manifesto involving the total liberation of the human being, in both bodily and spiritual aspects; it was the sovereign proclamation that God could not accept the death of the human being, the poor and the rich, the weak and the powerful, the hungry and the sated."[11]

The theology of Luke, "the evangelist of the poor," is not sectarian. Jesus, who came "to announce the good news to the poor" (Luke 4:18), upon arriving in Jericho, made a point of staying, not in the house of a poor person, but rather in the house of Zacchaeus, "who was rich": "Zacchaeus, be quick and come down; I must come and stay with you today" (Luke 19:5). And he was not an honest rich man, but "a chief tax collector," in other words, one of the exploiters of the poor and collaborators of the Roman oppressors, who were the "imperialists" of that time.

Jesus is a universal man and a free man. He breaks with all religious, political, and ideological systems. In response to the murmuring of those who accused him of "being a guest in the house of a sinner" (19:7), Jesus proclaims: "Salvation has come to this house today—for this man too is a son of Abraham" (19:9). And Luke concludes the episode in these words: "The Son of Man has come to seek and save what is lost" (19:10).[12] Liberation from sin is possible only through God's forgiveness; and this forgiveness is offered freely to all human beings, without exception, who are receptive, with repentance and faith, to the liberating love of God, a love which creates a new existence in the human being.

Having said this, it is unequivocally necessary to reaffirm with the same clarity that liberation from states of socio-economic oppression is an essential, inalienable part of the good news proclaimed by Jesus; and furthermore the poor who suffer the consequences of that situation are the privileged recipients of that good news. From the standpoint of our study (and because of mistaken emphases which have led to spiritualist misinterpretations, with detrimental practical effects that are well known), we stress the second aspect. But we are by no means denying the first. Furthermore, the second aspect, that is, the liberation of the poor, the hungry, the afflicted, and all those who are suffering, will be possible only to the extent that the first, that is, liberation from sin

and selfishness in the heart of human beings, takes place whether
explicitly or anonymously.

Evangelical Liberation in the CEBs

How is the good news of the liberation of every human being,
proclaimed by Jesus, achieved; that is, how has it become a reality
in the CEBs which accept the gospel? In the final part of our study,
we shall attempt to answer this fundamental question more completely. Here, we shall cite just one example. The individual
church in the prelature of São Félix (Mato Grosso) explicitly de-
fines its pastoral mission as liberating evangelization, according
to the words of Isaiah (61:1–2) which, as we have just observed,
Jesus used to define his mission. Jesus addressed primarily the
poor, the afflicted, and the hungry, as attested in the most ancient
version of the Beatitudes, preserved for us in Luke's account. According to the "programmatic discourse" delivered at the Nazareth synagogue, the purposes of Jesus' mission are "to evangelize the poor," "to proclaim release for prisoners," "to recover
sight for the blind," "to let the oppressed go free," and "to proclaim the year of the Lord's favor" (Luke 4:18–19).

This proclamation of the good news to the poor cannot be identified with a socio-political program. The CEBs in São Félix, like
thousands of other communities scattered throughout Brazil,
consider themselves communities that desire to live in accordance
with the demands of the gospel. And the gospel cannot be subjected to any socio-political programming or ideology. What the
CEBs want is to make a reality "here and now" in each community
of the process of liberation begun in a totally irreversible manner
by Jesus. What the local church of São Félix, "challenged by
the local reality," wants in particular is to make a reality of the
salvation-liberation outlined by Jesus in the "now" of the prelature's territory.

The analysis of the local situation shows that the people of the
region are a people oppressed in many ways: "superstition, fatal-
ism, and apathy; illiteracy and semi-literacy; social alienation;
and the capitalist hacienda system, responsible for the perpetua-
tion of this state of oppression."[13]

In view of this situation, the response given by the evangelization team was "to start and accelerate among the people of the

region the process of total liberation with which Christ liberated us (Gal. 5:1),"[14] a commitment which is leading to the liberation of the people from the bondage that has been cited. This commitment has become a concrete act of liberation, using the following three means of pastoral action: "(1) [incarnation] intimately entering into the people's poverty, struggle, and hope; (2) liberating education, through conscienticization and human development programs; (3) prophetic denunciation."[15] These means used by the local church of São Félix to achieve evangelical liberation with and by the poor are in fact also used—depending on the different requirements of each concrete situation and depending on the degree of consciousness attained by each community—in all the poor communities receptive to the gospel that are mentioned in the reports, although they are not depicted and explained in such a clear-cut, incisive manner.

Incarnation in the People's Poverty, Struggle, and Hope

The local church of São Félix bases its option for the oppressed and with the oppressed, doctrinally, on the gospel and the teachings of the Church, particularly those in the documents from Vatican II and the Medellín Conference. In fact, we can find the theological grounds for the first means listed in the widely publicized preface to the Pastoral Constitution on the Church in the Modern World. In order to remain faithful to its calling to announce the message of salvation to all human beings, the Christian community must feel truly a part of the history of humankind. A Church which intends to be a true community of Christ's disciples must achieve solidarity with "the joys and hopes, the griefs and anxieties of today's human beings, particularly those of the poor and all the afflicted" (GS 1). In other words, in order to preach the gospel truly and effectively to the poor, the Church must achieve solidarity with the poor and become incarnated in their poverty.

The gospel is the preaching of the reality of God's love for human beings. Its efficacy is demonstrated in actions and deeds in the service of brothers and sisters that are the continued incarnation of God's love in Jesus Christ, throughout the history of the "persons whom God loves." To attempt to cultivate the gospel in airtight compartments, dissociated from the real lives of human beings, is to make it fruitless. On the other hand, when the gospel is taken seriously, when it is "heard" and "obeyed" within the lives, the entire lives of those committed to it, it is "converted" and "shifted" in the direction of God's plan for salvation, to its "convergence" point: the building of fraternity among human beings in Jesus Christ. The consequences of faith in the gospel and of conversion to the gospel are immediately apparent. The lives of Christians who have been converted and committed to the good news of liberation become a risk, and a constant struggle.

In this respect, the CEBs are in a privileged situation: the evangelizers share the lives of those to whom the gospel is preached. The gospel is not something that comes from outside, culturally. It is a seed which sprouts from the ground of their suffering and oppressed lives and which breaks the hardness of that ground precisely because it is rooted therein. The evangelizers are not more protected socially, economically, or politically than the other members of the community. They suffer the same oppression, the same persecution, and the same torture as well.*

There can be no evangelization without incarnation. The poor Christians in the CEBs, through their lives that are intended to be lived in obedience to the gospel, through the defense of their rights and their acts of solidarity with and in the service of their brothers and sisters, through their suffering and persecution as a result of the gospel, bear witness to the truth and efficacy of their faith, their hope, and their love. This is how those Christians are evangelizing and building the Church, the people of God, in the forests, the hinterland, and the settlements of the interior. Those CEBs, which are almost always anonymous, are vitalizing the Church of Jesus Christ; they are the salt of the earth and the light of the world.

Liberating Education, through Conscientization and Human Advancement

Preaching the gospel to the poor of the CEBs means, specifically, preaching that God wants salvation-liberation (for each one

---

*Translator's Note: At various times torture became a common practice of police and military agencies in Brazil. Priests, religious and laity were not spared this experience.

of them and their communities) from the state of oppression in which they find themselves. For them, the state of oppression is, concretely, the expulsion of the squatters from their land, the exploitation of the farm hands on the large estates, illiteracy, disease, and hunger; and the lack of jobs, schools, and hospitals. An evangelization which did not preach the liberation of the region's people from this kind of oppression, denouncing its causes, would be a pseudo-evangelization; it would be a misrepresentation and perversion of the gospel, because it would virtually negate what constitutes the very center of the good news: the reality of the love of God which liberates the poor, oppressed, and afflicted. Failing to denounce these situations, out of fear or self-interest, would mean an intention of corrupting God's love. Now the love of God for human beings (with everything resulting from it, often anonymously) is the only absolutely incorruptible reality in this world.

The first step in eliminating such situations is the consciousness of their injustice, and their disgraceful and intolerable contradiction to God's will for salvation. The interpretation of these situations in the light of faith has, in fact, led the members of the CEBs to discover that they are in flagrant contradiction to the gospel.

The liberating education, through conscientization and human advancement, carried out in the prelacy for the purpose of prompting the people "to take a critical position toward the reality, and to undertake a social change which will make the real life experience of the gospel possible," is described in the report from the Ribeirão Bonito and Cascalheira communities as follows:

Group studies based on the gospel, courses for adults, meetings of mothers and young people concerning specific problems, community health work, and personal contacts are the activities which prompt the people to gather, discuss their problems, unite, find solutions, and direct them toward their total liberation. We attempt to engage in these activities in response to the wishes of local groups, and these activities are involved with the reality. For example, the courses are based on the history of the people from the region, and their purpose is to lead the groups to develop a critical sense, acquire an awareness of the reality, become capable of analyzing it, and be converted into promoters of social change. In the health-related activity, in addition to rendering assistance, insofar as we are able, to these people deprived of any assistance in this area, we are attempting to use it as a tool for creating a greater consciousness of their reality and their rights.[16]

Those CEBs are evangelized and evangelizing entities because, in them and through them, the gospel is proclaimed, discovered, and lived, with its most drastic demands. To the members of these CEBs, the gospel is a concrete commitment to liberation and a constant appeal for conversion, "the saving power of God" (Rom. 1:16). The power of the gospel reunites human beings, destroying the dividing walls, destroying selfishness, and also slowly destroying the oppressive politico-economic structures. It creates solidarity and fraternity, it causes the emergence and growth of courage and hope in the hearts of the poor and a consciousness of their dignity and of their rights as children of God.

When the activities of the CEBs are examined even with little theological depth, the radicalism, dynamism, and evangelical balance with which the communities have actually surmounted an entire series of artificial obstacles, without complicated theories, are impressive. The CEBs have not succumbed to secularism nor spiritualism; they cannot be realistically accused of either horizontalism nor verticalism; and they are neither conservative nor progressive. They maintain the two extremes of the arc of Christian existence in a fruitful, dialectical tension: spontaneous prayer and liberating action; explicit living experience of faith and work for human advancement; sacramental celebration of salvation, and its continuation in the liturgy of life, in the "sacrament of the brother and sister." They achieve even what is most difficult: the struggle for justice and liberation, without surrendering their rights when faced with threats and persecution, and without succumbing to hatred for their oppressors.

Prophetic Denunciation

This third type of pastoral action was the one which made São Félix famous throughout all of Brazil, and even outside of the country.[17] Denunciation is the other aspect of the preaching of the good news. The gospel is, simultaneously, salvation (for those who accept it) and condemnation (for those who reject it). No one can tear out the pages of the gospel which are bothersome. At times one finds side by side on the same page the Beatitudes and the threats (compare Luke 6:20–23, with Luke 6:24–26), luxury and poverty, agony and consolation (Luke 16:19–31), and blessings and curses (see Matt. 25:31–46).

It is impossible to proclaim the gospel of Jesus Christ as an announcement of conversion and salvation, as a real transition from sin to grace, from darkness to light, and from captivity to liberation, without denouncing what sin, captivity, and death are. As a result of these denunciations members of the São Félix church have been slandered, threatened, persecuted, tortured, exiled, and even assassinated. But this is how it makes up what is lacking in the Passion of Christ; this is how it announces the death of the Lord until he comes; this is how it celebrates the Paschal victory of the Lord, which is the transition from captivity to liberty and from death to life. In short, this is how it gives witness to the gospel.

The preaching of the gospel in the form of witness and martyrdom has always bothered the "great" and "powerful" of this world because it is the public denunciation of injustice, arrogance, ambition for power and for wealth at any price and by all means, and the denunciation of "progress" constructed with the sweat, hunger, and blood and with the short lives and many deaths of the poor.[18]

However, the denunciation of injustices is not the direct and primary goal of evangelization. It is (as we have said), the other aspect of the announcement of liberation outlined by Jesus Christ.

For Christians who want to live their faith with at least a minimal amount of consistency, the announcement and denunciation must result in an involvement in the battle for the construction of a more just, more humane, and more fraternal world. This is why human advancement is an essentially integral part of adherence to the gospel, and hence of evangelization. This battle is demanded by real love (God's and ours) for human beings subjected to injustice. Anyone who does not love the alienated and the abandoned with an operative, liberating love does not, in fact, believe in the gospel of God's love and does not love God.

The Gospel According to Matthew and the CEBs

"Blessed are the poor in spirit,
for theirs is the kingdom of heaven" (Matt. 5:3, RSV)

While upholding a proposition which "runs counter to the most generally accepted interpretation,"[19] Dupont concedes that Matthew introduces into his writing of the Beatitudes a reinterpretation that is not "spiritualist," but rather spiritual: "Blessed are the poor in spirit" (5:3), "blessed are those who hunger and thirst for righteousness" (5:6, RSV); "blessed are those who are persecuted for righteousness' sake" (5:10, RSV). As we have remarked previously, there is good reason to believe that Jesus devised the Beatitudes reiterating the prophecy in Isaiah 61:1–2. Then was Matthew, in his version of the Beatitudes, unfaithful to the meaning that they had in the preaching and mission of Jesus?

It is now generally accepted by exegetes that the Gospels are not neutral and strictly "objective" reports of the words and actions of the historical Jesus. It was the evangelists' intention to lead the readers to an understanding of the meaning that the words put in Jesus' mouth have for Christians in the concrete situations in which they find themselves, and which do not coincide exactly with the situation surrounding Jesus' preaching.[20] In the final analysis, this application to the new situation is more faithful to Jesus' intention than a mechanical faithfulness to the letter of his words.[21] The consecutive interpretations of the Beatitudes are not mutually destroyed because of the fact that they are different. The announcement of the joy proclaimed for the poor is as real in the sense and context of Jesus' preaching as in the sense and context of the Christian communities for which Matthew was writing.

"The poor in spirit" in Matthew 5:3 cannot be merely identified with the "humble" and the "little people." Matthew did not "spiritualize" Luke. Both had the same fundamental concept of the poor, which originated in the Old Testament, particularly in Deutero-Isaiah and the Psalms, through a long evolution. The poor whom Matthew proclaimed as blessed were also socially and economically alienated and oppressed.[22] The difference between Matthew and Luke lies in emphasis. Particularly after the exile, the *anawim* are, in particular, the "religious ones," those who await salvation from God alone. But it was through a long, painful experience of economic and social oppression and alienation (and not because of a naturally religious disposition) that they were prompted to trust and hope in God alone as their liberator and savior. It is this consciousness of the *ani*, who does not count or carry any weight in society and who has neither a voice nor a chance, that is expressed, for example, in Psalm 40:17: "But I am poor and needy; O Lord, think of me. Thou art my help and my salvation; O my God, make no delay." In Matthew, these *anawim* who are poor "in the most deep seated and most concrete aspect of their condition, in the eyes of human beings and in the eyes of God,"[23] are proclaimed as blessed. Matthew stresses this total attitude of humility which stems from a state of economic and social humiliation, whereas Luke places more stress on the aspect of privation, oppression, and humiliation which the poor suffer because of their material poverty.[24]

Returning to the question that we asked at the beginning of this section: Was Matthew, in his version of the Beatitudes, unfaithful to the meaning that they had in the preaching of Jesus? We respond: Jesus' original message did not lose any of its validity and timeliness, as we shall note subsequently when analyzing how the good news of the Kingdom proclaimed by Jesus is fulfilled among the poor of the CEBs. The updating done by Matthew for the Christians of Syria in the decade of the eighties is still, however, evangelically associated with and liberating for the poor Christians of today. Jesus himself was personally an *ani*: "poor in spirit, meek, humble, and patient" (see Matt. 11:28–30, and also 12:17–21 and 21:5). "The ideal of humility was wonderfully adapted to the image of the Messiah from Isaiah 40 ff."[25] Jesus, in his conduct as Messiah of the poor, pushes to its ultimate consequences the attitude of humility in the eyes of God and in the eyes of human beings.[26]

The Mystery of the Kingdom is Revealed
to the Little Ones (Matt. 11:25-27)

   This path that he traversed is the same one that he proposed to
the disciples who wanted to enter the Kingdom. Jesus praised the
Father (confessing and acknowledging = *exomologuein* [Gr.]) for
revealing the mystery of the Kingdom, the mystery of his person
and his mission as manifested in his words and actions, to the
"simple ones" (*nepioi* [Gr.]), to the ordinary people who are disdained as "ignorant, blind, and foolish" by the "learned and
wise" (Matt. 11:25). In the religion of the Law, the privileged ones
are the "doctors of the Law." Jesus made a 180-degree reversal;
he made the last first, he made those disdained as "ignorant and
blind," because they did not know the Law, the privileged recipients of the Kingdom.[27] However, here also, "the reason for the
privilege of the *nepioi* should not be sought in either their simplicity or ignorance, nor in the inclinations of their hearts resulting
therefrom; it lies in the *eudokia* (Gr. approval) of the Father, and
in the Father's totally gratuitous benevolence toward them."[28]
"Yes, Father, such was thy choice" (Matt. 11:26).
   The *eudokia*, the approval of God is paradoxical: "The al-
mighty God is close to those who are little."[29] The Kingdom be-
longs to the "little ones." This "Gospel according to Matthew"
must also be preached to the Christians who belong to the CEBs
and who are "poor" and "little ones." The CEBs are swept by with
a breeze of joy and liberty, because in them the simple people
from the interior, without losing their simplicity, hear, wonder,
and accept in faith, hope, and love, that, through the benevolence
of God, they have been chosen to know the mysteries of the
Kingdom of God, and that they have been chosen for the liberation and salvation planned by Jesus. These poor people, while
being evangelized, are simultaneously evangelizing us; they are a
living appeal for our conversion to the gospel. If we assume an
attitude of evangelical truth, if we want to be servants according
to the gospel and not manipulators of the poor in the CEBs, if we
are willing to respect them evangelically, without trying to make
tools of them and dominate them for the sake of "a prioris" in
contradiction to what constitutes the very heart of the gospel ac-

cording to Matthew, we shall discover that the Christians of the
CEBs in Brazil are living almost spontaneously (with a spontaneity
which results from the action of the Father's grace and approval).
And they want to live even more truly Jesus' example of humble,
unassuming service to each other, with mutual forgiveness, fraternity, and active rejection of violence; in short: love for one's
neighbor. And among the synoptics, Matthew's Gospel is the one
which most emphasizes this love as a distinctive trait of the disciples of Jesus.

"What do the basic communities seek?" asks José Comblin.
And he answers in his typically direct and incisive language: "Essentially, they seek charity; that is, they want to rediscover what is
most central to Christianity and to put the Church back into the
life that is lived daily again. Anything else is secondary; and if we
want to understand the meaning of the basic communities movement, we must maintain absolutely that this is what they are seeking, and nothing more. It may happen, incidentally, that they
would sometimes dwell on other matters; but on such occasions
they would let themselves be distracted from what, thus far and at
least in Latin America, is their very conscious goal."[30]

After all, what are the CEBs? They are places of communion,
where the presence of the Kingdom of God, which is a kingdom of
justice, peace, and love, is manifested sacramentally, that is, visi-
bly and effectively. They are communities of poor people who are
living, and trying to live increasingly, faith, hope, and love. This
incarnation is as simple as it is radical, and as fragile as it is transforming. It is in the nature of the incarnation of the Word in the
flesh of humankind. "In fact, the experiences of the basic communities are experiences of what is most elementary and most
simple in the human being."[31] And for this very reason, paradoxical though it may seem, they are something completely new for
the Christians who comprise them. As the reports demonstrate,
the majority of them had never before had the experience of a
personal and communitarian encounter with the gospel; it had
never been considered among them, and the strength of its unity
had never before been experienced.

The CEBs in Brazil are and want to be increasingly communities
of faith, prayer and worship, and charity; small communities in
which the Gospels are read or heard, and reflected upon; in which

there is community singing of the same faith and hope, in which one learns to love, forgive, and serve; in other words, converting that faith and hope into a practice of liberation.[32] The faith which has been discovered and intensified in the CEBs is a "faith active in love" (Gal. 5:6). The Christians in the CEBs, who are zealously seeking what is good and who often suffer for the cause of justice, are accounting for, with their words and actions, the hope that has been placed in them (1 Pet. 3:13–15). Out of their poverty, each day they experience the efficacy of their faith, hope, and charity, which in their lives are really "virtues," powerful forces which are increasingly liberating them from the cycle of dependence, abandonment, ignorance, disunity, and despair which was oppressing them more and more. They are actually participating in the transformation of the world, by transforming the relations among themselves and their relations with the world of labor, economy, politics, and culture, through an evangelical ferment. They do not seek to be revolutionaries; they are living the permanent revolution of fidelity to the gospel in their history.

"You have my Father's blessing;
come, enter and possess the kingdom" (Matt. 25:34)

Matthew, who in his version of the Beatitudes expands the concept of the poor in comparison with Luke, explicating it still further in texts such as 11:25–27, carries the Messiah's solidarity with the poor, interpreted in the strong sense that the term has in the Bible, to unsurpassable extremes in the passage concerning the Last Judgment. "When the Son of Man comes in glory," at the end of the world, he will emerge defending all human beings who are defenseless, definitively (seated on his throne) discharging the typical function of the ideal king that had been prophesied by Isaiah for the time of the Messiah and introduced into the "today" of the programmatic discourse given in the Nazareth synagogue. Furthermore, on the occasion of the great judgment, according to Matthew, the Messiah will be identified with all human beings who have objectively suffered deprivation of the most basic necessities: with those who suffered hunger and thirst, with the aliens and exiles, and with the naked, the sick, and the imprisoned (see Matt. 25:35–36). All these poor people are the same unprotected, alienated, despoiled, and oppressed to whom Jesus announced liberation during his earthly ministry. Now, on this occasion, "describing the transition from the hidden, preached Kingdom of God to the Kingdom manifested at the end of time,"[33] the Son of Man reveals, "in the presence of all nations" (25:32), that is, to all human beings of all times, that the defense of the defenseless and the good news of liberation proclaimed formerly to the privileged of the Kingdom is fulfilled through a self-emptying, and a maximum solidarity and identity of the liberating Messiah with the most wretched of all human beings.[34]

Matthew does not remove the temporal quality of the eschatology, confining it to mere ethics. "Matthew's ethics remain thoroughly eschatological, in the temporal sense of this term, both here and in Chapters 5–7 and Chapter 18."[35] Matthew cites the coming of the Son of Man "to underscore the 'ultimate' importance of acts of love, that is, of help in the service of the littlest ones."[36] The Last Judgment is not described for its own sake, but rather to give grounds for and uphold the appeals for active, merciful watchfulness which mark the entire narration of Matthew."[37] Just as he did in his entire Gospel, Matthew emphasizes here the importance of doing: what counts in the Last Judgment "is not intentions, or feelings, but acts of assistance."[38]

What the faithful in the CEBs are seeking is to live in charity, impelled by the dynamism of charity. They do good because it is good to do good. Regarded as crude and ignorant and despised by the powerful, they unpretentiously serve the "little ones," all the needy, whether they are Catholics or not. The situation of people who are naked, hungry, sick, without rights or protection, without liberty, and oppressed, is the "normal" situation among the poor of the CEBs. By serving their poor brothers and sisters, the Christians in the CEBs are effectively proclaiming the good news of the liberation of the poor. Therefore, at the end of time there will be revealed in their works the reality of the Kingdom, which is now hidden (perhaps even from their own eyes), but really present.

The Gospel According to Paul and the CEBs

A reading of the information concerning the poverty and alienation of the Christians comprising the CEBs[39] immediately calls to mind the passage from 1 Corinthians 1:18–31, in which

Paul contrasts the wisdom of God and the wisdom of this world. The community founded by Paul in the cosmopolitan and densely populated port of Corinth, during a year and a half of preaching, consisted for the most part of Christians who belonged to the lowest classes of the populace, although there were also some well-to-do people (see 1:16; 11:17–34).[40] Similarly, among those who have accepted the call from God in Brazil today and have joined the CEBs, "few are wise, by any human standard, and few are powerful or highly born" (1 Cor. 1:26). The faithful who comprise them are from the forgotten people of the interior and the outskirts of cities. In the interior one finds poor colonists, small landholders, immigrants from other regions, sharecroppers, manual laborers working on farms and making charcoal, and hands from livestock ranches engaged in a subsistence agriculture, using primitive, rudimentary implements, the vast majority of whom are illiterate. On the outskirts of the cities there are slum-dwellers from the hills and mangrove swamps, the high areas and the ravines; underemployed, doing odd jobs, and unemployed; small wage-earners, small business owners, lower ranking civil servants, construction workers from hod carriers to mechanics including plumbers and electricians; domestic workers, laundresses, and seamstresses.

It is in the hearts and the social environment of these men and women, elderly and children, youths and adults, that the seed of the gospel has been planted. And the seed is producing fruit, because it is good ground for the gospel. And the seed from that fruit is making new poor communities flourish, which, in turn, are producing new fruit of the same evangelical species. What gospel is this? The same one that Paul preached in Corinth: the gospel of the power and wisdom of God, manifested on the cross of Christ; the gospel which is intolerable folly and scandal to the great and powerful and to the wise and just "of this world"; the gospel which saves by destroying to the point of annihilation the strength of the strong, the power of the powerful, the justice of the just, the wisdom of the wise, and the intelligence of the intelligent, making them nonsense and stupidity in the eyes of God (see 1 Cor. 1:18–20)—because "God chose to save those who have faith by the folly of the Gospel" (1:21), and because "divine folly is wiser than the wisdom of humans" and divine weakness

stronger than human strength" (1:25). Those who believe in this
gospel and are saved are those who are receptive to the power of
God, confessing their inadequacy and poverty; they are those
who discover the paradox of the grace, wisdom, and power of
God, manifested in the cross of Christ. Paul observes in the cross
of Christ the fundamental symbol of salvation worked by the
power of God. It is at the same time the symbol of and the path to
the reality and the fulfillment of the Kingdom. The cross ex-
presses the Gospel according to Paul with maximum intensity.[41]
Paul never expressly mentions the Kingdom of God as the content
of the gospel, but the gospel that he preaches is precisely the proclamation of the manifestation and the operative reality of God's
power and saving justice, in the event of Jesus Christ and the faith
of those who accept it. To Paul, the "now" of the Kingdom is a
present and future reality which, as a result of the power, justice,
and mercy of God in Jesus Christ, operates in the *Ekklesia* [Greek
church], among the messianic people.

In the existence and spread of the CEBs it has been shown once
again that the means used by God to lead human beings to salvation are not those of power, wisdom, or prestige, but rather those
of poverty, weakness, and the most drastic impotence in the eyes
of "this world." The folly of the cross continues to be manifested
in the preaching of the gospel to the poor, and in its acceptance by
the poor.

The poor, the alienated, those with neither an opportunity nor a
voice in the eyes of the great ones of this world, accept the gospel
because they have been chosen by God. Paul's emphasis on this
paradoxical choice is impressive: "What the world counts folly[42]
God has chosen to shame the wise; and to shame what is strong,
God has chosen what the world counts weakness. God has chosen
things low and contemptible, mere nothings, to overthrow the
existing order" (1 Cor. 1:27–28).[43] "You are in Christ Jesus by
God's act, for God has made him our wisdom; he is our righteousness; in him we are consecrated and set free" (1:30). "Being in
Christ Jesus" has an emphatic meaning here: Those regarded by
the "world" as "low and contemptible" through God's choice become the conveyors of the new existence in Christ Jesus, the only
ones who really exist, with the only type of existence that has
stability. "The new human being will not be made by the powers

that have possession of the world. That human being will emerge from the common person, without power. At least this is what Christian faith means. The role of Christianity consists of remaking the human being from the bottom, and rebuilding from what is weakest and most lacking."[44] In the reports from the CEBs which we are studying, there is a delineation of the most fundamental traits of the new human being, and the new humankind.

The main purpose of the CEBs is not to make their members rich, nor to produce goods, but rather to create priceless values and types of human relations and coexistence which are in keeping with the Christian dignity of the human being. Everyone participates actively and consciously in the selection of goals and tasks that are necessary for attaining those objectives. The work done by the community, conceived as a community service, is really for the community, and not just for a few.

The forty-four rural CEBs in Barreirinhas[45] are an impressive witness to the timeliness of the "Gospel according to Paul," the gospel which is God's strength in the weakness of human beings. The Christians who now belong to these communities have always been considered by the faithful of the diocese as ignorant, incapable of thinking, to be despised, and almost inhuman. Today, they are a constant, painful, disturbing, and scandalous challenge to the Christians of the diocese:

> Every day, members of those forty-four CEBs traverse the streets of the main city of the diocese. They discuss their worship, debates, community work, apostolic visits, and Bible discussion groups. They express enthusiasm for the faith. They evoke admiration for some of their heroic deeds, recounted with the greatest simplicity, for example: covering hundreds of kilometers on foot, swimming across rivers, and going from one settlement to another to explain the format of the CEBs in the Church; combining voluntary representatives from five CEBs to visit another neighboring CEB which is divided into two opposing factions, in order to help it discover the path to its unity and peace; confronting scandal in its own milieu and creating a solution, by persevering in mutual discussion and prayer; appearing en masse to select the board of directors of the rural union, despite the organization of a terrorizing police apparatus, etc.[46]

Those once despised are now challenging their former masters through their many great achievements related to faith, through their hope, perseverance, and creative dynamism, which will liberate them from a state of social, economic, cultural, and religious alienation that is regarded as constitutive, inevitable, and irremediable. The poor of the CEBs in the rural area and some of the fishing villages of Barreirinhas are giving witness to the liberating force and efficacy of the gospel, more through their deeds and actions than through words. The faithful of the urban part of the diocese have been "judged," they are in a state of "crisis" (and they are confused and disturbed, without knowing how to extricate themselves) owing to the evangelical and evangelizing existence and action of the rural CEBs. In this regard, "the so-called traditional Church has not forgiven the so-called Vatican II Church for its lowly and disdained condition, which caused it to lose power."[47] In fact, the Church in Barreirinhas today no longer has the power, influence, and social prestige that it had formerly; and this has completely disoriented the Christians of the urban center, leaving them without a capacity for initiative.

> Without suspecting it and hence without a conscious intention and only because it shares its faith openly, each CEB is making a genuine revolution in its respective settlement. The members, gathered in autonomous assemblies, without the priest in attendance, are finding the joy of discovering the truth and, through it, liberty and love. They read the Bible at worship, and apart from it, and derive from it divine accounts, principles of lofty wisdom, and the mysteries of Christ and his view of the Kingdom. They discuss those treasures together, in contrast to the tragedy of their daily human lives; and thus the first pentacostal revolution is made. Each one makes the transition from knowledge received to knowledge discovered. In an extraordinary manner, each one experiences self-revelation: of personality, capacity for free action, and even an obligation to create history, at all times due to the experience of a knowledge that has been discovered and verbalized.[48]

The author of the report clearly discerns the economic weakness of the rural CEBs in Barreirinhas. Part of a broader socio-economic context, over which they have no control, they are probably doomed to death, "unless a miracle happens."

> The rural CEBs are extremely vulnerable. They are weak from an ontological standpoint; for either they are desperate residents joined together in a last attempt at survival in their place of origin or, as the CEB members themselves testify, it is God's doing. In any event, they have no stable existence and consistency by themselves. Those rural Christians are living a miracle. Through God's special intervention, these weak and humble people (from whom the rich and powerful remain aloof) are facing an impossible overall situation, and yet they are progressing. Deprived of all resources—cultural, social, economic, or political—nevertheless, with constant, widespread discussion, joined together by a strong love, steadfast in the faith, and explicitly invoking the name of Christ, with great effort they are attacking their own poverty, which is perhaps the most deep-seated in Brazil. The world of the forty-four CEBs, the Barreirinhas countryside, is probably doomed to death. It lacks socio-economic and cultural conditions for surviving the invasion of capitalist civilization which is being brutally imposed. It has no capital, resources, voice in the society, or technology for cultivating the land. The forty-four CEBs will die—unless there is a miracle.[49]

This prospect (with this anxiety and this blessing, the report concludes) calls to mind Jesus Christ, cut down by the power of his time; it recalls the primitive community of Jerusalem, dispersed by persecution, and the Church of Saint Augustine of Hippo, annihilated by the barbarians. Perhaps the forty-four CEBs will be demolished by a raging whirlwind and their remains scattered over the four corners of this vast country, Brazil, for other seeds and other harvests (something which would not diminish the guilt of contemporary society). Meanwhile, like so many other churches of today and yesterday, the forty-four CEBs are writing in their own flesh and blood the gospel of our Lord Jesus Christ according to Barreirinhas, and blessed are they who read it with faith and devotion.[50]

There are but few communities that have received the grace of an "evangelist" to preach to those who are far away the force and efficacy of the gospel of the liberating Messiah. But what is important is the fact that this gospel exists and, while the rich and powerful are unreceptive to it, the poor accept it.[51] These facts prove to us that the gospel message "brings with it a wisdom that is not of this world. It is able to stir up by itself faith—a faith that rests on the power of God (1 Cor. 2:5)" (EN 2). The gospel according to Paul of Tarsus, reaffirmed by Pope Paul VI, is being heard by the poor of the CEBs and is working miracles in their lives.

V

HOW THE GOOD NEWS OF THE KINGDOM PROCLAIMED BY JESUS IS FULFILLED IN THE CEBs

---

What Became of the Hope of the Poor?

The central, dynamizing, and constructive core of Jesus' message is the announcement of the coming of the Kingdom: "Jesus came into Galilee proclaiming the Gospel of God: 'The time has come; the kingdom of God is upon you; repent, and believe the Gospel' " (Mark 1:14–15). In Luke's Gospel, Jesus himself identifies his mission with the proclamation of the good news of the Kingdom of God: "I must give the good news of the kingdom of God to the other towns also, for that is what I was sent to do" (Luke 4:43; see also 8:1, and parallel texts). This mission of Jesus, which is explained in his public ministry with words and signs, applies to his entire life, from birth to death. Therefore, his birth is an *evangelion* (Gr. good news), good news of great joy coming to the whole people (Luke 2:10).

As has been demonstrated previously, Jesus considered the most characteristic feature of his mission to be the proclamation and fulfillment, through words and signs, of the liberation of the poor. In the first section of Chapter I of the apostolic exhortation, *Evangelii Nuntiandi,* Pope Paul VI comments on and summarizes Jesus' witness regarding his mission, as described in Luke 4:43 and 4:18, in these words: "Going from town to town, and proclaiming, particularly to the poorest people, who were often the most willing to accept it, the joyful announcement of the fulfillment of the promises and the Covenant made by God: such is the mission for which Jesus claimed to have been sent by the Father" (EN 6).

A little further on, in an attempt to "depict the meaning, the content, and the modes of evangelization, as Jesus conceived it and put it into practice" (EN 7), Paul VI writes: "Among all the other signs there is the one to which he attaches great importance: the humble and the poor are evangelized, become his disciples, and gather together 'in his name,' in the great community of those who believe in him" (EN 12).

After twenty centuries, what became of the liberation of the poor? Can the preaching of the gospel of the Kingdom be today, as it was in Jesus' preaching, the good news for the socially and economically oppressed? Can the coming of God's Kingdom be announced to the poor, those who are in fact poor, those who are suffering the unjust oppression of the rich, the powerful, and the violent, as good news which will actually bring about an end to their sufferings? This is a serious question, the most serious one that could be asked of Christianity after twenty centuries of history, because it stems from what constitutes the very heart of the gospel of Jesus. Are the prophecies in Isaiah's Book of Consolation, which became "today" in the person and mission of Jesus, continuing to be fulfilled in the history of those who accept his message and become his disciples? Are the poor, in fact, what they are inalienably through evangelical right, namely, the privileged recipients of the Kingdom? Can they be truly evangelized; that is, can the good news of liberation be preached to them truthfully and effectively?

Poverty: An Ideal or an Evil?

Before proceeding further, so as not to embark on the blind alley of an idealizing and moralizing interpretation of the good news preached to the poor, we must pause for a few moments to answer a question: Is poverty an ideal or an evil?

Throughout the entire Bible, a dialectical tension is maintained between two aspects of poverty: On the one hand, it is a scandalous situation that is insufferable to the justice and mercy of God; on the other hand, it is a privileged state for an encounter with God, for receptiveness to God, and for confidence in God.[1] It is obvious that the socio-economic poverty which humiliates and degrades the dignity of the poor is offensive and insufferable to the justice and mercy of God. God cannot and will not allow the poor person, who is in the divine image and with whom Jesus, the Messiah, is identified in a real way, to be oppressed, exploited, and wronged.

The poverty of the poor, in the strong sense of the biblical term, is a result and a manifestation of sin. How can one fight against that poverty, which is an evil because it is a result of sin? How can we embark on the dynamics of the dialectical tension, attested to in the Bible, whereby poverty is, simultaneously, insufferable to God and the path toward an encounter with God?

There is a series of converging attempts to respond: "Poverty can only be cured by attitudes of poverty. It is a disease which requires homeopathic treatment."[2] Poverty, "as an evangelical virtue, is the visible and accessible countenance of human service on behalf of those who suffer oppression and hunger, and the only possible guise for transforming the human family collectively."[3] Gustavo Gutiérrez seeks the synthesis by considering poverty "a commitment of solidarity and protest."[4] Poverty, when it is assumed voluntarily in the manner of Christ's making "himself nothing" (Phil. 2:6–11) and out of love for him, "is an act of love and liberation. It has a redemptive value."[5]

In his book entitled *Les pauvres et la pauvreté dans les Evangiles et les Actes,* Dupont demonstrates in a convincing way that poverty, as it is described indirectly in the Gospels and Acts when they discuss the poor, is not and cannot be an ideal; it is an evil which must be eliminated.

1. In twenty-one out of twenty-six instances, the term *poor* (or the plural form the *poor,* Gr. *ptochoi*) means people needing material assistance. Hence, poverty is not an ideal; it is an evil whose victims must be helped. The ideal proposed to Christ's disciples, and to all Christians, is not poverty in itself, but rather the exercise of charity, love that is lived, so that there will not be poverty in

the strong sense of the biblical concept. The gospel, when lived radically and in a communitarian manner, leads to the actual elimination of the scandal of socio-economic poverty.

2. The ideal of the "summaries" of Acts points in the same direction (2:42–47; 4:32–35).[7] The ideal community is one in which each person feels a sense of solidarity with everyone else, and in which each person has what is required to fulfill his or her needs. After studying these texts, Dupont reaches the following conclusion: "The ideal proposed by Luke in his description of the primitive community is not poverty nor abnegation, but rather a more simple and more profound ideal: fraternal charity. This is reflected, not in love for poverty, but in love for the poor. It gives an impetus, not to become poor, but to be watchful so as to prevent anyone from being in need.[8] Therefore, if we interpret the term *poor* in the strong sense given it in the Bible, the primitive community of Jerusalem was not and did not attempt to be a "poor Church," much less a "Church of the poor," but just the opposite: a community which, through the love lived and operating among its members, overcomes the injustices in the possession of material goods which cause poverty.

3. The fact that the state of suffering and oppression of the poor to whom Jesus preaches the good news of the Kingdom is not an ideal, and cannot in any way be idealized, has already been demonstrated previously: that state is insufferable for the justice and mercy of God and, for that very reason, God decided to put an end to it. The "message" which is addressed to us today, when we hear the proclamation of the good news of the Kingdom of God to the poor, is that we must love the poor as God loves them, with a preferential love that will liberate them concretely and historically from the unjust oppression which they are suffering. Anyone who does not strive to put an end to the suffering of the poor by becoming involved in their liberation is dissociated from and opposed to God's saving plan.

Mission of the Church as Perpetuator of the Mission of Jesus

The mission of the Church is to continue, throughout history, the mission of Jesus, the Messiah of the poor. If it wants to remain faithful to the mission entrusted to it, the Church must preach the good news of the liberation of the poor as what it is: the focal point of its message. To fail in this preaching is to betray its mission.

At Vatican Council II, the Church recognized its shortcomings in this area as well, although perhaps too timidly: The Church "is very well aware that among her members, both clerical and lay, some have been unfaithful to the Spirit of God during the course of many centuries. In the present age, too, it does not escape the Church how great a distance lies between the message she offers and the human failings of those to whom the gospel is entrusted. Whatever be the judgment of history on these defects, we ought to be conscious of them, and struggle against them energetically, lest they inflict harm on the spread of the Gospel. . . . Led by the Holy Spirit, Mother Church unceasingly exhorts her children to 'purify and renew themselves so that the sign of Christ can shine more brightly on the face of the Church' " (GS 43).

With this spirit of conversion and renewal, the National Conference of Brazilian Bishops (CNBB) addressing the ordinary people in particular, the "people from the basic communities and the study groups," admits:

There was a time when our preaching to the people advised mainly patience and resignation. Today, without ceasing to do this, our words are also addressed to the great and powerful, to indicate to them their responsibility for the suffering of the poor. The Church has attempted to take up the defense of the rights of the weak, the poor, the Indians, and the children yet to be born. Today, however, it no longer asks for the people an alms consisting of leftovers falling from the table of the rich, but rather a more just distribution of goods.[9]

The Church must follow the example of Christ. It cannot exclude anyone, and it must offer everyone, great and small, the means of salvation that it received from Christ. But its option and its preferred people are the weak and the oppressed. It cannot remain indifferent to the dispossessing of the Indians expelled from their land, or to the destruction of their culture. It cannot close its eyes to the serious state of insecurity in which the marginal classes live, or to the hunger of the poor and the malnutrition of children. It cannot ignore the uprooted or the migrants seeking new opportunites, who find shelter only under viaducts or who find shelter in slums, ghettos, or barrios, on the outskirts of the large cities. Christ is present and visible in these people. To mistreat them is to mistreat Christ.[10]

The grounds that this Pastoral Message to the People of God offers for the Church's option on behalf of the weak and oppressed and all those who "have neither a voice nor an opportunity" in the society are genuinely biblical:[11]

It is the poor and the defenseless who fill the jails and police stations, where there is frequent torture of victims who are there on charges of not carrying identification papers, or who are arrested during the dragnets of the police raids. Only the poor are charged and arrested for vagrancy. For the powerful, the situation is quite different. There are criminals who are not punished because they are protected by the power of money, prestige, and influence in the society which protects, and hence is an accomplice, in this type of injustice. This double-standard would appear to suggest that, in our society, it is only or primarily money, and not human beings, that is the source of privilege. At the assembly of the Bar Association, which convened recently in Bahia, the lawyers themselves expressed concern over this state of affairs, giving a reminder that, "Penal law is the law of the poor, not because it safeguards and protects them, but rather because it imposes the weight of its force and severity on them exclusively."[12]

The large business firms, equipped with legal and financial resources, are putting an end to the small property owners, and ousting the Indians and squatters from their land. These small property owners, small farmers, and squatters, who even have difficulty in obtaining an identity card, are unable to document land ownership, or to assert their squatters' rights before the justice system. So, they are ousted from the land and driven farther away, even to neighboring countries, or are converted into new nomads, doomed to wander through the byways of the country.[13]

In order to be faithful to its mission, the Church cannot, however, confine itself to a merely verbal proclamation of the good news of the Kingdom to the poor and to a denunciation of what is in flagrant contradiction to it. In addition to the announcement and the denunciation, which are always necessary, the Church must perform deeds and acts of liberation like Jesus who in his ministry proclaimed the good news of the Kingdom, not only in words, but also in actions which were "signs" and "proof" of the presence of God's justice and mercy among human beings. In the preaching of Jesus, the Kingdom is not announced as an extraterrestrial future, but as a reality that is already present and acting in history.[14]

"Signs" of the Presence of the Kingdom among the Poor of the CEBs

God's plan of salvation, revealed definitively in Jesus Christ, continues to be manifested and concretized historically as salvation and liberation, mercy and consolation for the poor and unfortunate, so long as the Church, the messianic people and the sacrament of salvation, moved by the Spirit of the Lord, performs acts and signs of justice, mercy, and love toward those who have nothing to eat or wear, or no place to live, and toward all the indigent, oppressed, and unfortunate, whether they be its members because of faith and baptism, or are beyond its visible borders. This is what is happening at present in thousands of CEBs scattered over the length and breadth of this vast country. The poor Christians who comprise them live on faith and hope in the coming of the Kingdom, struggling with the poor but always efficacious resources of the gospel to overcome the state of dependence, oppression, and even misery in which they find themselves. The Church, which they are, effectively manifests the presence of the Kingdom among human beings when the poor, dispossessed, and abandoned people of those communities are received in the Church as if it were their own home; when the poor who comprise those communities become conscious of the fact that they are the children of the Kingdom, a Kingdom of truth and justice, love and peace; and when those poor people, accepting the good news, are prompted by faith, hope, and love to perform concrete deeds and acts of justice, liberation, and salvation. Following are some examples of how the good news of the Kingdom proclaimed to the poor of the CEBs has been received, lived, and witnessed.

The Christians in the CEBs of Linhares, seriously and as a community, question the concrete problems that they experience in the light of the gospel. The word of God is the force which prompts them to confront those problems that are preventing them from living with the dignity of children of God.[15] In the Espírito Santo community, consisting of forty families, all of whom are black, there are five study groups which meet weekly in homes to reflect on the problems of their lives in the light of the Bible.[16]

The gospel, the good news of liberation, has often been used throughout the history of the Church as a means of oppressing the poor. A poor community which acquired a consciousness of its situation in the light of the gospel expressed it thus: "No one was born to die. We need to emerge from a religion of fear to a religion of salvation, from a religion of oppression to a religion of growth."[17] The following testimony, referring more explicitly to the action of the Spirit in the community and its result, unity, is in the same vein: "This work is bringing greater unity here and outside. Today, the people see that it is possible to do something; they have lost fear. The people learn to defend themselves in contact with others. I don't understand how it is done, but the people are doing so many things without knowing anything. They feel the strength of the Holy Spirit."[18]

At the assemblies in the diocese of Goias, there arose an awareness of a "poor Church for the poor." There was an option for the "evangelization of the alienated, through conscientization of faith." This conscientization of the real problems of the specific people living in the area of the diocese fostered and stimulated a community quest for the gospel[19] and was expressed a year later at an evaluation session as follows: "The option for the alienated has gradually evolved toward an option against the sytem of alienation." As the people discovered their social "declassification," they were aroused to a class consciousness which has been

expressed in various ways, attitudes, and statements.[20] The discovery of the gospel coincides with the discovery of unity and its
value, based on the will of the Father and the message of Jesus.
Joaquim, a semi-literate man with a prophetic quality, described
the strength of the unity and hope of the poor in this way: "The
most important thing is for the person to believe in it, because we
poor people are born and grow up believing only in others." This
unity, discovered in the CEBs and in the encounter with the gospel,
is not a closed, selfish, ghetto-type unity, but rather an open,
dynamic, and liberating unity, placed in the service of others. The
following comment by a farmer in the same report expressed that
idea: "Everything that we do for others, resulting from love for
neighbor, is appreciated by God and is related to pastoral activity." It is completed by another remark: "The good thing about
this movement of ours is that we feel like real human beings."[21]
The liberating innovation of the gospel which, when discovered
"for what it is," creates in those who accept it a new consciousness
and new attitudes, is reflected in this statement from the CEBs of
São Mateus: The general attitude of the people in the seventy
communities of the parish before they set out on the path was one
of acceptance and submission to the important families that took
advantage of their prestige and strength to oppress the poor.
"Some, the rich, must give orders; others, the poor, must obey."
Along the way, the poor discovered the gospel for what it is: the
good news proclaimed to the poor. This discovery is a source of
joy and energy which burst forth from within the community in
which the gospel is heard and obeyed and which edifies the community, spreading beyond its borders.[22]

The report from Itabira describes the accomplishment of the
housing project, carried out on Sundays using the cooperative
work system. Even the children collaborate, in an atmosphere of
solidarity, creativity, fraternity, and joy. There were many difficulties, but they were surmounted. "At this point, we are happy,
because we are not concerned only with a roof for the people; the
main objective is the formation of a community spirit and an awakening to others." Further achievements could be mentioned as
part of the same spirit: a mothers' club, a medical station, health
campaigns, improvements in the means of communication, and
the like. "The liberation brought by Christ occurs where the peo-

ple have a right to speak, judge, and act. That liberation does not exclude any area or sector of the entire human condition."[23]

In the Jales communities, the widest variety of community work is done, as a sign of incarnation of the faith among all the participants, for "the solution to the most immediate problems of the communities, such as those of schools, roads, health, care for the neediest people, construction of trading posts for the community, promotion of recreational activities, and participation in trade associations. All these problems have helped to make the communities grow. Ordinary people, without education, are proving their ability and worth in these activities. The farmers in particular have created a greater awareness of their strength as a consequence of the practical activity that they deduced from the gospel."[24]

The Christians in the Tacaimbó CEBs gave the most impressive report on the poverty and state of misery in which they live. But, in the midst of their miserable situation, something new occurred. Now they are conscious of their situation, and are having the experience of liberation. The analysis made by the members of the community themselves of the transition from captivity (the consciousness of "before," which becomes self-conscious only afterwards) to liberation (the consciousness of "now") is a wonderful depiction of the experience of liberty to which they were called and led by the discovery of the gospel and by obedience to the gospel: "The people live in a massacred state, and are used to that." When faced with all this, the poor feel downtrodden and go unnoticed except when they cast their votes for the rich. "Furthermore, the people live without being considered."

> The majority of the poor have little self-confidence or confidence in other poor people. The poor person always feels quite incapacitated for much of anything and always places trust in the rich claiming: "I am just leaning on a tree which provides shade." In fact, the poor often have little to do with other poor people.
>
> There are even some poor people who know something; they know how to read and to speak properly; but that does not help them much. All that one needs is to be rich, or even own four cows and be called a rancher. Even if such a person

knows nothing, many would back him, and even elect him
mayor. The poor person considers himself so small that he
does not consider one like himself to be any different. If
poor people would give other poor people a chance, things
might change. Thus far, this has not happened, and it would
be hard to achieve. The poor do not believe that they can
emerge from this situation in which they are living. They
cannot believe in improvement. They can only believe in
worse conditions until the end.

The poor person does not view politics itself as an improvement, but only as an occasion for receiving a favor,
which is almost no solution. So, many have no hope, and
content themselves with saying: Things are all right this
way; this is our lot; what more can people expect? There are
poor people who even like living in poverty. But there are
also some who have hopes of joining together to change
things. However, many think that without the rich, the poor
cannot survive; but the only way in which people cannot
survive is without the power of God. The majority of the
poor do not even know where to turn in this situation; the
expedient that they find is to appeal to God, but they are
wandering about, not knowing where they are bound.

People are now observing the poor uniting, but it remains
to be seen whether the unity is merely a pretense. The poor
person does not have a chance in the local society. The society is made for those who have prestige, those who have a
name, an education, or money. The little people have no
place in it. A better society for the poor has yet to appear. It
will occur when a poor person gets along well with others,
and, together, they become associated with one another.[25]

This new and growing consciousness of their rights and their
oppression has also changed the consciousness of the place of the
poor within the Church:

Not long ago, the poor had no place in the Church either.
The only ones who had a place were the powerful and the
strongest. The poor did not even have a chance to speak,
because the priest himself hushed them to remain silent.

There was no place for the poor in any choir, in the society, or in the Church. All discussions, and all the priests' personal associations, were with the rich. The poor had no rights. In order to speak to a priest, the poor had to speak to the rich person who was with him. Because of the people's innocence, they liked those times, and considered it normal for the priest to be the major personage in the Church. So, even in the Church, the poor were always demeaned. The Church that we knew a short time ago was the Church of the priest; the people did not speak or participate. There was not much difference between how the poor felt in society and how they felt in Church. People attended Mass, but they did not understand, they did not know what the priest was saying. Since we were brought up this way, my mother used to say: "No, my daughter, that is the place of the holy fathers; we were born to stay over here in our own place." No one would go near a priest except people who were crazy; they were scolded harshly. The people did not know how to read, they had no learning, they did not know what they were hearing, but every month they attended Mass.[26]

The discovery of the gospel caused the emergence of a new consciousness among the poor, and especially a new consciousness of being a Church, and of what the Church is: a Church in which everyone has the same fundamental rights, a Church that is the people of God, called by God without discrimination or exclusion of persons: "It is not only for the white, the black, the rich, or those with high rank; it is for everyone who wants to follow the path of God. The poor have the same right as the rich, and the rich must remain on the same level as the poor in order to belong to the Church." The Church is no longer viewed as the property of the priest, a Church in which the people remain silent and impassive. These are the signs of the presence of the Kingdom: those who were silent now speak, those who were discredited now participate, and those who felt rejected, alienated, and sad, now feel joyful, liberated, and the "hosts of the feast." In the past, the feast of São Antonio was for the rich: "Now, the feast is for us who are poor, all united; there is none of that business of rank; we are all together. Now we think that we are in a different life, we are free in this respect, we are all hosts of the feast."[27] The poor are "the hosts of the feast," but not egotistically. Their joy is spread and conveyed to others. Starting with the feast, other kinds of unity appeared; houses were constructed for the homeless, work was done in the outlying areas. "This unity is spreading. We were waiting for this unity, and this work, and for our liberation. We were in captivity in this respect, and now I myself feel free, and I hope that everyone will have this liberty."[28]

The paths of liberation for the poor are long and perilous. But the experience of liberty and communion, hope and faith, rooted in the hearts of the poor by the discovery of the gospel, is capable of surmounting the obstacles that seemed to be insurmountable in the past: "Manuel of São Benedito, who is almost unknown here, had his clearing invaded by forty men, sent by a powerful local ranch owner who destroyed it. There were twenty-five farmers in Manuel's house holding a day of prayer. When the meeting began, the owner who invaded the property ordered the place destroyed. This provocation gave us the courage to back Manuel even more in his cause, which is now in the courts."[29]

The community of Sítio Granjeiro, in the parish of Mogeiro (Pernambuco), consists of poor farmers cultivating their small plots on the mountain heights. Four years ago, they discovered in the gospel that Christ came for the integral salvation of all, and the signs of the Kingdom have been becoming visible in their daily lives. The process, initiated at the incentive of the priests, evoked the interest of instructors, leaders of prayers, and catechists. The means used for the discovery and practice of the gospel are the simple, effective means that the people now use: visits to residents at which there is shared reflection, cooperative projects in which the farmers work together, and study meetings. At these meetings, there is reflection concerning the problems of the farmers, their causes and their consequences, in the light of the gospel. When compared with the people's concrete problems, the gospel sheds new light on those problems. At the same time it is discovered or rediscovered as the good news of liberation, creator of friendship and communion, and of confidence and courage for coping with the problems jointly. When the reality is grasped and the laws behind it studied, action for the transformation of that reality begins, and the living community assumes responsiblity

THE GOOD NEWS FULFILLED

for matters ranging "from aid to the needy to concern for greater problems, such as labor unions and land." The path toward meeting the demands for justice and fraternity in the gospel is slow, demanding, and at times dangerous. But for the Christians of the community of Sítio Granjeiro, "the person of Christ is a real presence, and a dynamic aspect in everything," even (in particularly) when they are persecuted and imprisoned for their cause, for the cause of unconditional commitment to the construction of the peace and justice of their Kingdom.[30]

Since 1971 the guidelines for pastoral action in the Prelature of Acre and Purus have included projects for assistance, such as hospitals and schools, for an involvement, through the founding of CEBs and evangelization groups, in the situation in which the poor and alienated people are living. Enlightened by God's word, the people are gradually acquiring an awareness of the causes of the social imbalances, tensions, and injustices that they are experiencing, and are prophetically denouncing this situation.[31] Land is the most serious problem in the area. What is the attitude and action taken by the local Church of Acre and Purus with respect to this problem?

In the municipality of Sena Madureira, the purchase of rubber plantations by investors from the South has created countless land problems. Nor is it possible to remain indifferent to the constant arbitrary acts, ranging from mere expulsion from land, without the slightest compensation, to threats of death or the burning of homes of squatters and rubber-tree plantation workers. The Church engaged in an intensive effort for conscientization, distributing four hundred mimeographed leaflets containing the six basic points from the Catechism of the local church among the rubber plantations. This guidance calmed many people, preventing a mere naive abandonment of their land, owing to the information about their rights and the legal protection from the Land Statute.[32] The leaders of the rural workers' union, with over eight hundred families, were from this community of Sena Madureira.[33] The poor of the community themselves are the preachers of the good news of the Kingdom: "Countless evangelization groups are appearing in the rubber plantations, on the clearings along the river, in the community schools, and inside the town itself. In addition to the coordination team, there are about thirty monitors coordinating more than thirty evangelization groups from this community."[34] In order to debate the essential problem of land itself, the coordinators and leaders of the Basileia Community visited nearly three hundred parish families, making a survey of the socio-economic and religious situation. The leaders met with agents from the INCRA [National Land Reform and Settlement Institute], and devised a project involving the Catechism on Land Rights.[35]

The position of the Church of Acre and Purus is not sectarian, much less subversive. It is quite legal and attempts to be completely evangelical.[36] The gospel can be "heard" and "obeyed" only in concrete situations. The force of the gospel, of the evangelical action and acceptance of the gospel through faith, is always liberating, creating justice and communion. Where this force for liberation and communion is not operating, it is because the gospel has not been preached nor accepted as the good news of Jesus Christ. In order to be faithful to the gospel, the local Church of Acre and Purus must concern itself with the most important, concrete problems of the region's people, so as to seek a solution for them with the cooperation of all those involved. And the ones most involved are, in fact, the poor: the small farmers, the squatters, and the rubber plantation workers who are suffering the injustices personally.

The distained and oppressed poor, such as the Christians of the present rural communities in Barreirinhas have managed, through the discovery and living experience of the gospel in their lives and through unity with one another, to overthrow the commercial and political structures which had been oppressing them for generations. New leaders such as preachers, catechists, apostles, have risen from those communities. What are those facts if not the good news of liberation becoming a reality to them? The transition from a life marked by individualism, division, passivity, and irresponsibility to a new type of life with communion, cooperation, and service to others with joy, is described in the report as follows:

In the past, the settlements experienced passivity, individualism, brawling, celebrations marked by drunkenness and murder, homes devastated by infidelity, the abandonment of children, etc. Today, many CEBs have created a new lifestyle, wherein there is a predominance of intense desire for learning, prayer and relationship with God, care of the sick, esteem for moral life, the spirit of work, the habit of planning and executing projects jointly, the organization of sports and leisure activities, overall contentment (without resorting to liquor), deep mutual love often manifested in forgiveness for offenses and public reconciliation, penitence with public confession of sins, steadfast attitudes toward threats from outside, the elimination of petty politics, solicitude for the neighboring CEBs, etc.[37]

Historical Liberation and the Fullness of the Kingdom

What are these facts if not the fulfillment of the promises of the Beatitudes and of the reality of God's Kingdom, insofar as it can be made real now in history? Its eschatological fullness will be created from all these acts of Christian love that the grace of God will transform finally into the new creation.

The Pastoral Constitution of Vatican Council II *Gaudium et Spes* states that on the new earth which God is preparing as the fullness of the Kingdom, love and its fruits will endure. "What was sown in weakness and corruption will be clothed with incorruptibility." What will disappear will be "creation's enslavement to vanity" (GS 39).[38] The relevance of struggle, in the form of dedication and service to brothers and sisters, for the accomplishment of the fullness of God's Kingdom is expressed by the Council shortly thereafter as follows: "After we have obeyed the Lord, and in his Spirit nurtured on earth the values of human dignity, brotherhood, and freedom, and indeed all the good fruits of our nature and enterprise, we will find them again, but freed of stain, burnished and transfigured. This will be so when Christ hands over to the Father a kingdom eternal and universal" (GS 39).

We deem it fitting to dwell a little longer on this point, one of fundamental importance to spirituality, in other words, to the concrete type of Christian experience in the CEBs. In the first place, as the Council tells us, "earthly progress must be carefully distinguished from the growth of Christ's Kingdom" (GS 39).

The Kingdom of God transcends history, in the sense that it is a gift of God from on high; and when it comes in its fullness, it will bring with it the end of history. We do not know when or how the transformation and consummation of the world (see GS 39; Acts 1:7) into the new heaven and the new earth which will be the final dwelling place filled with communion of human beings with God, and of human beings with each other, will take place. The coming of the fullness of God's Kingdom is not in the hands of human beings, but is rather a gift of God. Furthermore, the fullness of "life," of "holiness," of "grace," of "justice," of "love," and of "peace" (I interpret these concepts in all their biblical abundance) on the "new earth" will surpass all the aspirations of the human heart (see GS 39 and 41).

However, the transcendence of the Kingdom does not mean that human history is insignificant or indifferent with respect to the fullness of that Kingdom. The Kingdom of God is not a future world totally dissociated from the world in which the human beings of today, with their victories and defeats, live and struggle. The history of the salvation which will result in the fullness of the Kingdom is achieved, that is, it becomes a reality, within human history, and not apart from it. The Kingdom of God will be achieved through the working of the grace of God acting in the hearts of human beings and in the heart of the world. The preaching of the good news of the Kingdom of God, the privileged recipients of which are the poor, causes the creation, in the hearts of those who accept it with faith, of a hope which, in a perpetual eschatological tension, is reflected in works of charity and in an untiring commitment to all types of service. The measuring rod of this service is the potential or actual achievement of justice, peace and liberation proper to the Kingdom of God.

The Christians of the CEBs are obviously not concerned with the theoretical formulation and solution to the problem (which is theologically as important as it is difficult) of the relationship between earthly hopes and eschatological hope. They resolve it in their concrete existence, living a "faith active in love" (Gal. 5:6). Sharing the "joys and hopes," and the "suffering and anxieties" of all human beings, especially those of their poorest brothers and sisters, the Christians in the CEBs preserve faith and hope in the total and absolutely freely given love of God; and they remain faithful to the tasks demanded by evangelical love, which is service. They thereby eliminate the dualism between "religious life" and "secular life," a harmful dualism which destroys both the life of faith of those who claim to be Christians and the credibility of that faith in the eyes of non-Christians, and which was therefore so persistently and forcefully condemned by the Council.[39]

What became of the good news of liberation proclaimed to the poor by Jesus? We asked this at the beginning of this chapter. The hope of the poor will not be confounded. Indeed, it has to undergo the eschatological tension introduced into God's plan for salvation by the death and resurrection of Jesus, the Messiah. The Kingdom of God, which burst forth in an irreversibly victorious manner in the life, death, and resurrection of Jesus, will now, until the Parousia, be a *regnum cruce tectum* [kingdom covered by the cross]; but it is still present and acting in history. We do not know when its fullness will be manifested; but we know that its truth, justice, and liberty will become a reality as the rights of the poor and the weak are defended against the rich and powerful and as the latter are effectively prevented from oppressing the former.

Preaching the gospel to the poor means awakening in them faith and hope in the justice of the Kingdom. When those "bent low" by oppression hear the good news of the Kingdom as a proclamation of liberty, based upon the justice and mercy of God toward them, and accept it in faith and hope, this good news will become a force and a ferment within them that will, in fact, liberate them and spread the process of liberation.

VI

CEBs: FROM HEARERS TO PREACHERS OF THE GOSPEL

In the midst of that vast throng of poor people among whom the CEBs have been established there is being created, through the force of the Spirit, a Church in which the poor are, simultaneously, the evangelized and evangelizers, the privileged recipients and the conveyors of the good news of the Kingdom of God. Among the farflung messianic people, the CEBs are one of the places where one can breathe more deeply and purely the air of hope in the justice and mercy of the Kingdom of God which is absolutely vital to the Church. It is not an apathetic, alienating hope, but rather the strong hope of the poor.[1] Instilled with this "hope against all hope," the CEBs are trying to live, in a demanding way and under the extremely difficult conditions of their environment, the good news which they have accepted, celebrating it jubilantly in worship and proclaiming it courageously to those who have not yet heard it.

Can the Poor of the CEBS Evangelize and Liberate the Rich?

The evangelization of the poor, as practiced in the CEBs, will not only liberate them from the various forms of economic, social political, cultural, and even religious alienation in which they find themselves. It can also liberate the rich and powerful from the enslavement to power and money which they have reached through the injustice and violence practiced against the poor.

"The conviction that *wealth and poverty are equally bonds* from which human beings must liberate themselves or be liberated is essential to Christianity. But let us not forget that these two realities are not merely symmetrical. The human being pursues wealth, but succumbs to poverty. The poverty-stricken feel their condition like a weight and a chain; while the rich are almost never convinced of the bonds of their possessions."[2] Now the gospel proclaims, and its acceptance achieves, not only the liberation of the poor from poverty, but also the liberation of the rich from *pleonexia* [avarice] and the insatiable thirst for gain. In this connection, we can speak, like Father Pedro Arrupe, the Superior General of the Society of Jesus, about those "alienated below" and those "alienated above." In fact, in the eyes of faith, the chains of affluence (of *mammona iniquitatis* [Lat., mammon of iniquity]) enslave human liberty and dignity as much as the chains of poverty, if not more so.

Here we are faced with an extremely important evangelical problem, about which it seems to us that there is an urgent need to reflect. Without exceeding the bounds of our study, we shall note a few clues for theological reflection which should be probed more deeply. The Church today is often accused of opting for the poor as opposed to the rich, or at least of disregarding the latter. The argument then goes on to say that the gospel is for everyone. The evangelically irrefutable response to this objection has already been given previously: the gospel, and the liberation and salvation that it brings, must actually be preached to everyone without any discrimination. However, the "privilege of the poor" is at the very heart of the gospel proclaimed by Jesus.[3]

How can we reconcile these two assertions, which are equally peremptory, but which seem mutually exclusive? The fact of the evangelization of the poor, as it is occurring in the CEBs, offers us a clue for seeking the answer.

The example of Zaccheus and other public sinners about whom the Gospels speak shows us that, in the theocratic society of the Jews who were Jesus' contemporaries, the rich could be socially marginalized and were, in fact, when they were also viewed as public sinners. In our society, no rich person is socially marginalized, at least in the sense commonly attached to the term. But, in the light of the gospel (and even from a merely "humanist" view-point), the rich who accumulate their wealth, prestige, and power from the sweat, tears, and blood of the poor in the rural and urban areas who are forced without consideration to the sidelines by the socio-economic system in which they are not allowed to participate actively and freely, those rich are, in the light of faith, genuine "public sinners." Their sin must be denounced with the forcefulness that is in keeping with the seriousness of the violence and oppression that they impose on the poor. Therefore, the out-cry of the poor is perhaps the most effective means at present to announce to the rich the demands of the gospel. In any event, it is a type of evangelization which the Church cannot relinquish without betraying its mission as a faithful servant of the gospel.[4]

More specifically, how can the oppressed liberate their oppres-sors? They can do so by taking possession (evangelically!) of the gospel, of which they are literally, by divine right, the owners.[5] This appropriation is, in fact, taking place among the poor of the CEBs. By being receptive to the gospel which is preached to them, and accepting it in their own lives, they are acquiring a deeper consciousness each day of their dignity as children of God and of the liberty to which they were called. As this consciousness be-comes a historical practice of liberation, they will also liberate those who alienated them, even against the will of the latter.

More concretely, the poor who discover their dignity as children of God, and who strive together to liberate themselves from living conditions that are in flagrant contradiction to that dignity, also include the rich in the same liberation process. Just as there is a dialectical relationship between the oppressed and the oppressor, and the former cannot exist without the latter, there is also a dialectical relationship between the elimination of oppres-sion and the elimination of the oppressor as an oppressor. As the poor of the CEBs accept the gospel with all its demands, they are in fact creating the conditions for liberating the rich, first, from their pharisaical good conscience and their middle class ideology, which have caused them to regard the poor as "lazy," "vagrants," or "outcasts." In reality, the poor are not outcasts, but rather marginalized, and by-products that have been by-produced by an evil process of production and distribution. The content of these assertions has not been taken from Marxist ideology; it is as ancient as the content of the preaching of the Old Testament prophets.[6]

When the gospel is read from the point of view of the poor, there arises a Church made up of "a people who wrest the gospel from the hands of the great ones of this world (who now consider themselves its private owners), and thus prevent its being used to justify a situation that goes against the will of the liberating God."[7] That Church of the poor, which is born of faith in the gospel and conversion to the gospel, presents to the rich that gospel as it essentially is: the absolutely impassioned and intransigent defense of the rights of the poor, founded upon the justice and love of God. Those who hear its message and its denunciation, and who are converted to it will be saved. Those who selfishly close their ears and hearts will be condemned. What is at stake here might be expressed incisively as follows: whereas the oppressed poor person, strictly and scandalously speaking, would not need to emerge from poverty in order to be finally saved by the justice of God's love, the rich person can be saved only by ceasing to oppress the poor. Therefore, when the oppressed poor accept the gospel as good news of liberation, and actually strive to become liberated from the oppression that is being suffered, they are, ipso facto, battling against the sin of the oppressor, inviting the latter to conversion, and are making the greatest gesture of Christian love toward the latter. It is in this paradoxical way that the poor of the CEBs proclaim the good news of liberation to the rich who are oppressing them.

The CEBs Are Evangelizing the Church

The poor of the CEBs are not only proclaiming the good news of liberation to other poor people who have not yet heard it and, in a different manner, to those who are the direct cause of their oppression. They are also, and primarily, evangelizing the Church, from which they received the gospel, through witness to the force of their faith, the courage of their hope, the efficacy of their love, and the living experience of fraternity. The CEBs are for the Church and primarily a constant, pressing appeal to conversion.

"The Church is an evangelizer, but it begins by evangelizing itself. . . . It has a constant need to be evangelized, if it wants to retain its freshness, vigor, and strength in order to proclaim the Gospel" (EN, 15). We believe that the CEBs, with their evangelical poverty and simplicity, generosity and courage, constitute a genuine *kairos* [Gr. right occasion] and an authentic time of grace for this evangelization of the Church which Paul VI mentions. When we come in contact with the poor Christians of the CEBs, having even a minimal degree of evangelical concern and sincerity, "our false security and our illusions vanish like snow in the sun; the splendid and rather futile existence that we would build appears to us to be rhetorical and spurious. It becomes evident that we knew nothing: we were hollow, and could not even pass ourselves off as novices."[8]

A Church that fails to evangelize the poor, and that is not evangelized by the poor might be respected by the middle and upper classes and "become established" and have "prestige" and "influence" in society, but it would not be the Church of Jesus Christ. Communities that are disturbingly possessed of and dynamized by the messianic hope have as one of their charismatic functions the uncomfortable and always necessary task of "subverting" the arrangement and status quo in society and the Church—in the Church as well, because it is, at the same time, although from a theological standpoint not to the same degree, a "holy and sinful people."[9] The poor of the CEBs, as the indigents they are, are not prisoners of the ideologies of the "established order," nor of hollow "doctrines" and "traditions." Involved in reality, they point to new paths for their Church, removing it from its ruts, and leading it to a better harmony with the logic of the gospel.[10]

The great revelation of the gospel of Jesus Christ and the radical innovation of the good news that he brings lie in his preferential love for the poor and for sinners. When confronted with the CEBs of the interior and the outskirts of cities, the local churches, the diocesan Churches, and the Universal Church are challenged, and invited to the conversion that constitutes the very heart of the ministry and mystery of Jesus. The Church, the community of the Messiah, must follow the path of its Lord: seeking service, and not domination, a service aimed primarily, out of pure grace, at the poor and sinners, a service born of love, spurred on by love, which is for that very reason liberating. This love which in solidarity becomes service to the oppressed and will unfailingly lead the Church along the path of its Lord: poverty and persecution. The *agape* [Gr. fraternal love] of the Father is revealed in love for all those whom the "world" despises, alienates, and rejects. That revelation must continue in the Church, so that it may be, in fidelity to God and to human beings, increasingly clear as a sacrament, in other words, a visible true, effective "sign" of the universal, saving love of God for human beings.

The CEBs are demonstrating with deeds what was affirmed at the beginnings of Christianity by Paul, with unsurpassed forcefulness, and confirmed on constant occasions throughout the history of the Church: the force of the gospel, the saving power of God, is manifested in the poverty and weakness of human beings. This is what is happening among the Christians in thousands of CEBs scattered all over Brazil: in discovering or rediscovering the gospel as the good news of God's justice and mercy, they are discovering or rediscovering the liberty, generosity, and joy of Christian fraternity,[11] the force of communion in faith, hope, and love, which is what gives them courage and perseverance in their difficult struggle against the forms of oppression which degrade their dignity as children of God. "For the first time in centuries, there is in the Church a movement that takes seriously poor men and women, without power and culture, or rather, possessing only the culture and power of the poor. If charity and its proper expression are to emerge anywhere, will it not be from those basic communities?"[12] It will not be by trusting in the resources of "power," of "politics," or of "technocratic" *aggiornamento* that the Church will be faithful to its mission to preach the gospel. All these means end up stifling the Spirit, the giver of the evangelical spirit, typified by confidence in weak and fragile resources. Only with this fidelity to the Spirit, who anointed and sent the Messiah to evangelize the poor, will the Church be able to give witness before human beings to the good news of which it is the bearer and servant, at the command of its Lord.

NOTES

Introduction

1. "Thus, the basic Christian community is the first and fundamental ecclesial nucleus which, on its own level, must make itself responsible for the richness and expansion of the faith, as well as of the worship which is its expression. This community then becomes the initial cell of the ecclesial structures and the focus of evangelization, and it currently serves as the most important source of human advancement and development" (Medellín Document on "Joint Pastoral Planning," No. 10).

Chapter I

1. We cite the following three works as representative: Yves Congar, *Pour une Eglise servante et pauvre* (Paris, 1963); Paul Gauthier, *"Consolez mon peuple"*: *La Concile et l'Eglise des pauvres* (Paris, 1965); G. Cottier, J. C. Baumont, et al., *Eglise et pauvreté*, Unam Sanctam, No. 57 (Paris: Du Cerf, 1965). On this topic, see the article by M. D. Chenu, "Vatican II and the Church of the Poor," in *The Poor and the Church*, ed. Norbert Greinacher and Alois Müller, Concilium 104 (New York: Seabury, 1977), pp. 56–61.

2. AAS (Acta Apostolicae Sedis), 1962, p. 682.

3. Paul VI is more correct when he states that the poor are linked to the Church through evangelical entitlement. See Gauthier, *"Consolez mon peuple,"* p. 26. We quote from the Portuguese translation.

4. The great scandal of the Church in the nineteenth century—the loss of the workers' world, constituting the world of the poor in the new industrial society which arose in the West—still exists.

5. Editorial from *Informations Catholique Internationales,* No. 177, October 1, 1962. Although it is obvious, it is nevertheless appropriate to note that not all the statements in the editorial, which was written from a North Atlantic perspective, apply to the Church of Latin America, the vast majority of whose faithful are poor.

6. Quoted by Gauthier, *"Consolez mon peuple,"* p. 221.

7. Congar, *Pour une Eglise servante et pauvre*, p. 10f.

8. Chenu, "Vatican II and the Church of the Poor," p. 57.

9. See the summary made by R. Rouquette in *Etudes* "De Roma et la chrétienté," 316 (February 1963), pp. 260-266. According to Rouquette, this address was the most daring and the ".most reforming of all those heard during the first session, possibly opening a new path" (p. 266).

70

10. "We will not respond to the truest and deepest demands of our time, nor to the hope of unity shared by all Christians if we treat the theme of the evangelization of the poor as one of the many themes of the Council. It is not a theme like others; in a way, it is *the* theme of our Council. If it is accurate to state, as has been done several times, that the purpose of the Council is to conform the Church to the truth of the gospel, and making it capable of responding to the problems of our time, we can claim that the fundamental topic of this Council is, precisely, the Church as a Church of the poor" (excerpt from the address quoted in *La Documentation Catholique*, March 3, 1963, col. 321).

11. In addition to the quoted address, see the radio-television speech of December 22, 1962, in *La Civiltà Cattolica*, 114 (1963/1): 285–286, and, in particular, the lecture on "Poverty in the Church," delivered at the Apostles College in Jounieh (Lebanon), on April 1, 1964, subsequently published as a Preface to the work *Eglise et pauvreté* (see Note 1), pp. 9–21.

12. See the excellent, full study by J. Dupont on this paragraph from *Lumen Gentium* "A Igreja e a Porbreza," in *A Igreja do Vaticano II* (Petropolis, 1965), pp. 420–452.

Chapter II

1. The few CEBs existing in urban centers have varying features. We might note, in passing, that this fact of the nonexistence of typically urban CEBs is challenging from a theological and pastoral standpoint (see A. Gregory, "Formas de presença a da Igreja em grande cidades," Research Report, CERIS [Religious Statistics and Social Research Center], Rio de Janeiro, 1975).

2. Some of the reports (18.8 percent) could not be used in preparing these data (see "Comunidades: Igreja na Base," Estudos da CNBB 3, São Paulo, 1974: 20). "By rural-urban community, we mean the ones located in districts that are generally poor, and at times dissociated from the main city or town, but whose basic economic activity is primary, either agricultural or extractive" (ibid. p. 21).

3. The CEBs in Volta Redonda are only ostensibly the exception that proves the rule: they are not peripheral geographically, but are sociologically (see SEDOC [Documentation Service], May 1975, Col. 1129).

4. Regarding the importance of socio-economic conditioning for the incarnation and living experience of the gospel, see the studies by M. D. Chenu collected in the volume *L'Evangile dans le temps*, Coll. Cogitatio fidei, 11 (Paris, 1964). "These poverty movements (which flourished during the Middle Ages) are always led by a new type of Christian, emerging from the new human condition introduced by economic and social evolution, and hence dissociated from the earthly trappings of an established Church. The evangelical clash is perceived in the specific situation, and those who are not involved in this specific situation remain insensitive to the evangelical appeals" (p. 393). In this regard, see also the points underscored in Michel Mollat's article, "Poverty and the Service of the Poor in the History of the Church," in *The Poor and the Church*, Concilium No. 124, pp. 46–55. The author, an expert on the subject of "the poor and medieval society," stresses the evangelical roots of the movements on behalf of poverty starting in the eleventh century: their true origin "was the desire to conform a newly-revived spirituality to the Christ of the Gospels. They certainly cannot be solely or essentially explained by economic factors" (p. 49). What prompted the poverty movements to address themselves to the poor was imitation of the examples set by Christ and the Apostles. However, the evangelical motivation for the option on

behalf of the poor and their way of life did not diminish the strength of the protest derived from those movements. In fact, "a challenge was being hurled at one manifestation of wealth and power after another—ownership of land, the force of arms, titles, influence, money, and even learning" (p. 50). Mollat, with history as a basis, also makes this observation which should never be forgotten, but always kept in dialectical tension with the force of a challenge inherent in the movements on behalf of the poor which are meant to be evangelically radical within the Church: "It became clear that no movement of poverty could succeed without episcopal authorization and without humility" (p. 53). We are personally convinced that this is one of the reasons for the "success" of the CEBs in Brazil to date.

5. The fact that millions of Brazilians from the interior and the outskirts of large cities are living in a state of absolute poverty has been officially and publicly acknowledged. Their status is described in an editorial in *O Estado de São Paulo*, of September 9, 1976, entitled "BNA [National Food Bank] para 25 milhões de famintos," as follows: "According to estimates made by Minister Nascimento Silva, a quarter of the Brazilian population—nearly 25 million persons—is in a state of absolute poverty, typified by total lack of food, housing, clothing, and hygiene. Those unfortunates, sick, undernourished, and ragged, vegetate in unhealthy or unproductive parts of the country, as well as on the outskirts of the large cities. There are 25 million people living in a state of chronic hunger, 25 million pariahs existing in this nation."

6. See SEDOC, October 1976, Col. 259–264. The italics are ours.

7. See SEDOC, November 1976, Col. 524–535.

8. See Bishop Moacyr Grechi (Prelature of Acre and Purus) "Comunidade de fé e homem novo na experiência do Acre e Purus": in *Revista Eclesiástica Brasileira* 34 (1974): 897 and 906. See in ibid., p. 899 ff., the data on the experimental CEBs, showing between 70 and 80 percent of the population of school age as illiterate. In 1974, the prelacy had nine established CEBs, eight in the embryonic stage, and two in the planning stage, as well as 191 evangelization groups.

9. SEDOC, May 1975, Col. 1119.

10. Ibid., Col. 1120.

11. Ibid., Col. 1107.

12. SEDOC, November 1976, Col. 481.

13. Ibid., Col. 558.

14. Ibid., Col. 559.

15. Ibid., Col. 546.

16. Ibid., Col. 547.

17. SEDOC, May 1975, Col. 1094.

18. SEDOC, November 1976, Col. 465.

19. SEDOC, May 1975, Col. 1102.

20. Ibid., Col. 1061 ff.

21. Ibid., Col. 1077 ff.

22. Ibid., Col. 1083 ff.

23. See "Pequeno relatório de uma experiência de visitas intercomunitárias na periferia de Vitória—ES," (mimeographed).

24. See SEDOC, May 1975, Col. 1095 ff.

25. Ibid., Col. 1112 ff.

26. Ibid., Col. 1113.

27. Ibid., Col. 1129.

28. Doc. 1–2.10 (mimeographed). The assembly was held in Itaici, from November 8 to 11, 1976, to study the topic "Parish and Basic Ecclesial Community."

Chapter III

1. In preparing this section, as well as Section 3, we used essentially the studies by Jacques Dupont, particularly: " A Igreja e a Pobreza," in *A Igreja do Vaticano II* (Petropolis, 1965), pp. 420–452; *Les béatitudes*, II: *La bonne nouvelle*, Coll. Etudes Bibliques (Paris 1969); "Les pauvres et la pauvreté dans les Evangiles et les Actes," in *La pauvreté évangélique*, Coll. Lire la Bible, 27 (Paris 1971), pp. 37–62 (in a bibliographical reference at the end of the article, the author cites his most important previous studies related to this subject); "Introduction aux Béatitudes," *Nouvelle Revue Théologique* (1976): 97–108.

2. See X. Leon-Dufour, *Vocabulaire de Théologie Biblique* (VTB) (Paris 1964), Col. 769–770; Gustavo Guttiérrez, *A Theology of Liberation* (Maryknoll, N.Y.: Orbis Books, 1973), pp. 291–293, with the bibliography indicated in the references.

3. Dupont, "Introduction aux Béatitudes," p. 100.

4. See G. Forza "L'annuncio di gioia ai poveri", *Riv. Teol. Mor.* [Journal of Moral Theology], 9 (1977): 62–64. In Job 24:2–12, we have an impressive description of the oppression experienced by the rural proletariat of the time (the sixth century B.C.): "Wicked men move boundary-stones and carry away flocks and their shepherds. In the field they reap what is not theirs, and filch the late grapes from the rich man's vineyard. They drive off the orphan's ass, and lead away the widow's ox with a rope. They snatch the fatherless infant from the breast, and take the poor man's child in pledge. (Verse 9) They jostle the poor out of the way; the destitute huddle together, hiding from them. The poor rise early like the wild ass, when it scours the wilderness for food; but though they work till nightfall, their children go hungry. Naked and bare they pass the night; in the cold they have nothing to cover them. They are drenched by rain-storms from the hills, and hug the rock, their only shelter. Naked and bare, they go about their work, and hungry they carry sheaves. They press the oil in the shade where two walls meet; they tread the winepress, but themselves go thirsty. Far from the city, they groan like dying men, and like wounded men they cry out." The situation of the poor is described by the prophets with no less realism and forcefulness; and we shall quote some of their by now classic texts subsequently.

5. See Dupont, "Les pauvres et la pauvreté," pp. 38 ff.

6. This is also the meaning of those "in need" in Acts 4,34: "For they had never a needy person among them"; and in 1 John 3:17: "But if a man has enough to live on, and yet when he sees his brother in need shuts up his heart against him, how can it be said that the divine love dwells in him?"

7. "Those who hunger," who are proclaimed blessed in the Beatitudes, are literally the "hungry"; or more forcefully and more precisely, the "famished," those who "have hunger," because they have been deprived of the food necessary to live, and lack the means of obtaining it (see Dupont, *Les béatitudes,* II, p. 88).

8. This same theology is effectively retrieved in Targum 5, 4–6 (see the commentary by J. Corbon in *Assemblées du Seigneur* 57 [Paris, 1971]: 46–52). The wisdom literature includes Job, Proverbs, Ecclesiastes, the Song of Songs, Ecclesiasticus (Ben Sirach), and Wisdom. The Psalms are sometimes included.

9. See (for the other texts quoted hereafter also) the notes in the margin of the Jerusalem Bible.

10. The thoughts, machinations, and actions of the "irreligious" are also described with remarkably suggestive intensity in these verses from the Book of

Wisdom, last of the Old Testament books and perhaps only one generation earlier than Jesus: Down with the poor and honest man . . . let us show no mercy to the widow and no reverence to the gray hairs of old age. For us let might be right! Weakness is proved to be good for nothing. Let us lay a trap for the just man; he stands in our way, a check to us at every turn; he girds at us as lawbreakers, and calls us traitors to our upbringing. He knows God, so he says; he styles himself 'the servant of the Lord.' He is a living condemnation of all our ideas; the very sight of him is an affliction to us, because his life is not like other people's and his ways are different. He rejects us like base coin, and avoids us and our ways as if we were filth; he says that the just die happy, and boasts that God is his father. Let us test the truth of his words, let us see what will happen to him in the end; for if the just man is God's son, God will stretch out a hand to him and save him from the clutches of his enemies. Outrage and torment are the means to try him with, to measure his forbearance and learn how long his patience lasts. Let us condemn him to a shameful death, for on his own showing he will have a protector" (Wis. 2:10-20).

11. On this topic, see N. Lohfink, "I profeti erano dei rivoluzionari?" in *I profeti ieri e oggi*, Col. Giornale di teologia, 16 (Brescia, 1967), pp. 31-55.

12. Possibly because of the dispute in which he was involved with the priest of Bethel, who reported him to the king as a subversive. See in this episode (Amos 7:10-17) the charges made against Amos and the explanation given by the prophet in his own defense.

13. In other words, with meanness, treating the poorest strata of the population harshly and unjustly and denying them their rights.

14. "Shame on the man who builds his house by unjust means and completes its roof-chambers by fraud, making countrymen work without payment, giving them no wage for their labor!" (Jer. 22:13).

15. *Lexikon für Theologie und Kirche*, I, 879.

16. See the entry "poor" in biblical dictionaries; for a more extensive explanation see Albert Gelin, *The Poor of Yahweh*, trans. Kathryn Sullivan (Collegeville, Minn.: Liturgical Press, 1964).

17. See, in addition to the texts quoted in the previous sections, Psalms 45:4-8; 72:1-7, 12-14; Proverbs 16:12-13; 25:4-5; 29:4, 14; Jeremiah 23:5; 33:15; Genesis 18; 19. For a reading of other texts, the notes in the margin of the Jerusalem Bible may be followed.

18. Dupont, *Les béatitudes,* II, p. 88.

19. Ibid., p. 140.

20. Dupont, "A Igreja e a Pobreza," p. 440 ff. Valuable testimony to this primary function of the king to ensure justice in his kingdom, and particularly to protect the rights of his subjects who cannot defend themselves, is the famous Code of Hammurabi. King Hammurabi (1728-1686 B.C.) is depicted in the prologue as "the religious prince" and a "God-fearing" person, called upon by the gods "to make people joyful," and to "cause justice to appear on earth, to eliminate evil and perversity, so that the strong might not oppress the weak." Similar remarks appear again in the epilogue: the goal of Hammurabi's endeavor was to lead the country along the path of justice, "so that the strong might not oppress the weak, to do justice to the orphaned and widowed, and to proclaim righteousness in the country." See the analysis made by Dupont throughout all of Chapter 2 of *Les béatitudes* II, of the Mesopotamian, Ugarit, and Egyptian texts, in which the practice of justice on behalf of the weak and poor, against the rich and powerful, appears as a typical function of kings and gods. In this connection, it is interesting to note two observations made by G. Forza in "L'annuncio di giora ai

poveri" (note 35): first, in ancient times there was a lack of "theorization regarding the social classes and revolution to bring power to those who are deprived of it by violence"; and second, the laws of Israel relating to the defense of the poor and the weak have a uniqueness with respect to those of the surrounding countries: whereas in Egypt, Babylon, or Ugarit, that defense was incumbent on the state, in Israel it was the entire society, and not only the established authorities, which had to defend the interests of the poorest people, and the motivation for this defense was always of a religious nature.

21. Hans Walter Wolff, *Antropología do Antigo Testamento* (São Paulo, 1975), p. 257; in Eng. see *Anthropology of the Old Testament,* trans. Margaret Kohl (Philadelphia: Fortress, 1975).

22. Dupont, "A Igreja e a Pobreza," p. 441 ff.

23. Ibid., p. 442. See therein Notes 67–73 for the texts from Isaiah in which the biblical concepts used by Dupont in the last sentence quoted appear.

Chapter IV

1. Dupont, "A Igreja e a Pobreza," p. 443. In note 74 the author observes that Jesus, when referring to the messianic promises in the Book of Isaiah, retains only what they say about the benefits given to the unfortunate, omitting the counter-' part: the vengeance that will befall their oppressors. See especially Isaiah 35:4: "See, your God comes with vengeance, with dread retribution"; and 61:2: "to proclaim a year of the Lord's favor, and a day of the vengeance of our God."

2. For what follows see Dupont, *Les pauvres et la pauvreté,* pp. 45–53.

3. Luke, who adheres to the Greek version of the Old Testament, makes some theologically significant omissions and additions (see Note 1 above and Notes 13 and 14 of E. Samain's article quoted below) from and to the text of Isaiah 61:1–3a. The following translation is taken from E. Samain, "Manifesto de Libertação: O Discurso-programa de Nazaré"; in *Revista Eclesiástica Brasileira* 34 (1974): 270 ff.

Luke 4:18-19	Isaiah 61:1-3a (LXX)
The spirit of the Lord is upon me because he has anointed me; he has sent me to announce good news to the poor.	The spirit of the Lord God is upon me because the Lord has anointed me; he has sent me to bring good news to the humble, to bind up the broken-hearted,
To proclaim release for prisoners and recovery of sight for the blind. "To let the broken victims go free" [Isaiah 58:6], To proclaim the year of the Lord's favor.	to proclaim liberty to captives and release those in prison;
	to proclaim a year of the Lord's favor and a day of the vengeance of our God; to comfort all who mourn, to give them garlands instead of ashes, oil of gladness instead of mourners' tears, a garment of splendor for the heavy heart.

4. The *evangelical* significance of Jesus' miracles does not lie in their "miraculous quality," but rather in that they are real manifestations of absolute hope for the abandoned and hopeless people of this earth. This theme might also be devel-

oped from the standpoint of our study. Regarding the problem of the "meaning" of the miracles, the comments made by J. I. González Faus, *La humanidad nueva* (Madrid, 1974), pp. 120–122, may be noted in a broader context.

5. See Dupont, *Les pauvres et la pauvreté,* pp. 48–50. G. Friedrich comments in the same vein in *Theologisches Wörterbuch zum Neuen Testament* 2: 715: "These final words ('the good news is preached to the poor') constitute the culminating point of the sentence"; as does E. Bammel, ibid., 6:930. "Jesus' proximity to this class of people [the oppressed and underprivileged social class] is so great that, according to J. Jeremias, the summary of the gospel and of all Jesus' preaching is not that the Kingdom, or salvation, has come, but rather that salvation has come for the poor, and for sinners" (cf. González Faus, *La humanidad nueva,* p. 87; see on pp. 87–112 of the same work a good description of this matter of Jesus' relationship with the abandoned).

6. See Dupont, *Les béatitudes,* II, 92–99, and Samain, "Manifesto de Libertação," 280 ff.

7. See, for example, the famous work by Albert Gelin, *Les pauvres de Yahvé* (Paris, 1953); in Eng. see *The Poor of Yahweh,* trans. Kathryn Sullivan (Collegeville, Minn.: Liturgical Press, 1964).

8. Dupont, *Les béatitudes,* II, p. 15.

9. Ibid., p. 16.

10. See Dupont, "A Igreja e a Pobreza," pp. 444–445.

11. Samain, "Manifesto de Libertação," p. 283.

12. See also Luke 15:6, 9, 24, 32, and Mark 2:16–17, wherein Jesus responds to the criticism made of him by the scribes: "He eats with tax-gatherers and sinners," in these words: "It is not the healthy that need a doctor, but the sick; I did not come to invite virtuous people, but sinners." Dupont comments: "As Jesus uses it, the expression 'those who are lost' should be interpreted in the spiritual sense; they are sinners, considered lost people who must be found, people who despair of eternal salvation and who must be saved from damnation" ("A Igreja e a Pobreza," pp. 444 ff.). In conclusion: "Hence the prerogative of the poor is not exclusive. It appears, rather, as a particular instance that is part of a more extensive whole: all misery, both physical and spiritual, is of concern to the mission of Jesus; all of it moves him to pity and reflection on God's tender solicitude and God's desire to manifest mercy that is freely given and superabundant" (ibid., p. 445).

13. SEDOC, November 1976, Col. 564.

14. Ibid.

15. Ibid.

16. Ibid., Col. 564–565.

17. Extensive documentation (up until 1973) on the pastoral action of the Church of São Félix was included in the special September-October 1973 issue of the magazine *Misión abierta* under the title "Una Iglesia que lucha contra la injusticia." The most publicized subsequent events, associated with the prelature, were the assassination of Father John-Bosco Burnier, and the accusations made against the prelacy's bishop, Dom Pedro Casaldáliga, which were published by the country's largest newspapers. See Teofile Cabestrero, *Mystic of Liberation: A Portrait of Bishop Pedro Casaldáliga of Brazil* (Maryknoll, N.Y.: Orbis Books, 1981).

18. "Therefore, we go about here with death at our shoulders" *Misión abierta,* p. 81). The topic of death appears often in the book (a kind of autobiography) by Dom Pedro Casaldáliga, *Yo creo en la Justicia y en la Esperanza,* Col. El Credo que ha dado sentido a mi vida (Bilbao: Desclée de Brouwer, 1975). An English translation has been published by Fides/Claretian. We quote only two passages: "Mato Grosso was, and still is, a lawless land. . . . The law was of the most strin-

gent and harshest type. Money and the '.38' were in command. Being born, dying, and killing: those were, indeed, the basic rights, the verbs conjugated with shocking ease" (p. 34). "There is more dying and killing than living. Here, dying or killing is easier, and more accessible to everyone, than living" (p. 39).

19. Dupont, *Les béatitudes,* II, p. 147.

20. "The first Gospel updates for Christians what Jesus said to his contemporaries" (Xavier Leon-Dufour, *Introduction à la Bible,* II [Tournai, 1959], p. 185); "Matthew is trying to show how one can and should be a 'disciple' of Jesus during the years 80–90" (Pierre Bonnard, *L'Evangile selon Saint Matthieu* [Neuchatel, 1963], p. 10).

21. Dupont, "Introduction aux Béatitudes," pp. 98 ff.

22. The expression "poor in spirit" means really poor. The dative *to pneumati* (Gr., in or of spirit) is equivalent to the dative *te kardia* (Gr., of heart), that is, pure of heart, or really pure. Both expressions are found in Psalm 34:18. (I owe this reference to my colleague Professor Selong.)

23. See Bonnard, *L'Evangile selon Saint Matthieu,* p. 56.

24. H. Borrat summarizes the explanations of this matter given by the exegetes J. Schniewind and K. H. Rengstorf as follows: "If Matthew places more stress on the internal aspect of poverty, and Luke on the external aspect thereof, it is not because the one has perceived only the former and the other only the latter, but rather because of the particular status of the reader of each Gospel. In Matthew's Church, there was a great danger of arrogance based on a religiosity that was sure of itself (Matt. 5:2 ff; 6:1 ff; 7:1 ff). Luke, on the other hand, saw his Church threatened by the world and its values (Luke 12:13 ff; 16:19 ff; 18:18 ff). In other words, Matthew is combating religious self-sufficiency, and Luke worldliness. Each evangelist has his own 'pastoral concern'; in each there is a preaching of the good news geared to his respective church" ("Las bienaventuranzas y el cambio social," in *Fe cristiana y cambio social en América Latina* [Salamanca: Sígueme, 1973], p. 219).

25. R. Kittel, *Geschichte des Volkes Israel,* III (Stuttgart, 1929), p. 692, 245, quoted by Albert Gelin, *Os Pobres que Deus ama* (São Paulo, 1976), p. 137; in Eng. see *The Poor of Yahweh.*

26. See Gelin, *Os Pobres que Deus ama,* pp. 136 ff, 170 ff.

27. See Bonnard, *L'Evangile selon Saint Matthieu,* p. 10. The religious alienation is, therefore (in a theocratic society such as that of Israel), also social alienation of these "little ones" who "do not know the law." It appears in all its virulence in the comment put by John (7: 49) in the mouth of the high priests and Pharisees: "As for this rabble, which cares nothing for the Law, a curse is on them!"

28. Dupont, *Les béatitudes,* II, p. 216.

29. Ibid., p. 127.

30. José Comblin, "As Comunidades de Base como lugar de experiências novas," in Concilium, No. 104 (Port. ed.), 1975, p. 457.

31. Ibid., p. 462.

32. See J. Marins, "Comunidades Eclesiais de Base na América Latina," in Concilium, No. 104 (Port. ed.) 1975, pp. 404-413.

33. Bonnard, *L'Evangile selon Saint Matthieu,* p. 364.

34. In discussing the nature of this mysterious solidarity of the Son of Man with the wretched, Bonnard observes in it an example of the idea, typical in Matthew, of "a *simultaneously juridical, real, and eschatological identification* between this Judge and the poor" (*L'Evangile,* p. 366, No. 1; the italics are the author's). On the same page, he quotes Theo Preiss: *La vie en Christ* (1951), p. 82 ff: "The Son of Man was in solidarity with all those who had an objective need for assistance,

whatever their subjective inclinations were. . . . The Son of Man sees his brother or sister in every wretched person. . . . His love as a shepherd of Israel seeks solidarity with all human misery, in its ultimate vastness and depth." "This is a sovereign gesture of an absolute king, a gesture which destroys any idea of the existence of some good in itself, or an abstract justice apart from him; it rather lends an infinite weight and a divine glory to the most humble gesture of love. . . . But, on the other hand, the Son of Man wants nothing for himself: With a no less sovereign authority, he does not want to be served except in his brothers and sisters" (ibid., pp. 85 ff).

35. Bonnard, *L'Evangile,* p. 367.

36. Ibid., p. 364.

37. Ibid., pp. 366 ff.

38. Ibid., p. 366. Anticipating the topic of the conclusion of our study, we wish to cite here a paragraph from J. I. González Faus, *La humanidad nueva,* p. 99: "Lately, we have witnessed a spectacular discovery of Matthew 25:31 ff, in which the human being's encounter with God includes identity between the Lord and the imprisoned, hungry, or naked brother or sister. But it behooves us to note now that Chapter 25 of Matthew does not stand alone. Although it has preserved for us the positive content of what matters in judgment, source Q has preserved for us another comment on its negative content: on what does not matter in judgment (Matthew 7:21–23 and Luke 13:25–28). On that day, many will flaunt a series of ostensibly impressive credentials; but neither the privileged position (Luke) nor wondrous works (Matthew) will be of any use. Both will hear: 'Out of my sight, you and your wicked ways!' The concept has been reversed: wickedness results from being among those with the status of irreproachable ones. The Church might well ask itself whether these words from the Gospel do not condemn it, and whether (when confronted with the impressive magnanimity of some who, nevertheless, do not believe) it will not be the one to give this excuse: 'Did we not prophesy in your name, and in your name perform many miracles?' "

39. See above, Chapter 2.

40. See Gerd Theissen, "Soziale Schichtung in der korintischen Gemeinde: Ein Beitrag zur Soziologie des hellenistischen Urchristentums," in *Zietschrift f. die. neutest. Wissenschaft* 65 (1974): 232–272.

41. The noun *euangelion,* which appears sixty times in Paul's writings, has two meanings: the act of evangelizing, and the content of the evangelization. The first aspect is fully explained (unfortunately in an overall unilateral manner, to the point of making it absolute) by R. Cabello, "El concepto de evangelización," in *Servir* 11 (1975): 30–44.

42. The term "folly" is used here in the pejorative sense of foolishness and stupidity given it by the wise and intelligent ones "of this world," and concretely signifies those who are simple, crude, and ignorant.

43. Also related to this theology of the paradox of God's saving grace in Jesus Christ is the text of 2 Corinthians 12:7–10, wherein Paul formulates the law of all evangelization, this time from the standpoint of the poverty and weakness of the apostle. Whatever its concrete significance may have been for Paul, the "thorn in the flesh" was viewed by him as an obstacle to evangelization. It thus becomes the symbol of the deep-seated impotence experienced by Paul in his mission as an evangelizer, the symbol of all the physical and moral provocations that he suffered for the sake of the gospel: weakness, shame, want, persecution, torture, attacks, disasters, anxiety, etc., some of which are enumerated in 2 Corinthians 11:23–29; 4:7–12; 6:4–10; and 1 Corinthians 4:9–13 (see Stanislas Lyonnet, *Initiation à la doctrine spirituelle de Saint Paul* [Toulouse, 1963], pp. 5–8). "But it is precisely

when the apostle feels his weakness most profoundly that the power of Christ itself 'rests on him,' just as, at another time, the glory of Yahweh 'rested' on the Ark of the Covenant, a sign of God dwelling among the people (Exod. 40:34–35; Num. 9:18, 22), and as the Word came to 'dwell among us': In the apostle, deprived of all human support, and strong in his weakness, the power of Christ itself became 'incarnate,' so to speak" (ibid., p. 7).

44. Comblin, "As Comunidades de Base," p. 463.

45. See SEDOC, November 1976, Col. 524–535.

46. Ibid., Col. 527.

47. Ibid.

48. Ibid., Col. 528.

49. Ibid., Col. 531, 533, and 534. To the last remark, with its reservation, "unless there is a miracle," we wish to add the profession of faith of the martyr to justice and charity, Father John-Bosco Burnier, contained in a letter written a week before his martyrdom, and read by Cardinal Paulo Evaristo Arns (Archbishop of São Paulo) at the funeral Mass: "In this world of fear and force, it will be a miracle if justice triumphs in the end; but miracles do exist" (*O Estado de São Paulo,* October 20, 1976).

50. SEDOC, Col. 534 ff.

51. "The people who enjoy 'social status,' accustomed to class discrimination, refuse to 'mix' with those who are disreputable" (SEDOC, Col. 521). The highest class in the Prelature of Acre and Purus is unwilling to accept that particular Church which clearly took the option of 'defending the right of the weak and the oppressed in accordance with the gospel command' (Bishop Grechi, "Communidade de Fé," *Revista Ecclesiástica Brasileira,* 34 [1974]: 907), because it is afraid of losing its own privileges (see ibid., p. 906). The same phenomenon has occurred in the CEBs of São Mateus (Maranhão): the Church is attended by a small number of people, all of whom are humble folk; while the authorities and the people with a certain social standing remain aloof (see SEDOC, November 1976, Col. 559). The very gospel preached by Paul, which is the strength of God in human weakness, is now being lived in the communities of a parish in Espirito Santo: "The wealthiest and 'highest' class refuses to mix with the more humble class" (SEDOC, May 1975, Col. 1094); "the more a group increases its capacity for critical consciousness and autonomy, the more the 'wise' ones, the people with a higher cultural and economic standing, dissociate themselves, making room for the 'nobodies' " (SEDOC, November 1976, Col. 464).

Chapter V

1. See the study by J. M. González Ruiz, *Pobreza evangélica e promoção humana* (Petropolis, 1970), in which this dialectical tension inherent in the biblical theology of poverty is explained.

2. Ibid., p. 99.

3. A. C. Comín, in the prologue to the study by J. M. González Ruiz (note 1), p. 10.

4. See *A Theology of Liberation* (Maryknoll, N.Y.: Orbis Books, 1977), pp. 288–302, especially 299–302.

5. Gutiérrez, *A Theology of Liberation,* p. 300 "If the ultimate cause of man's exploitation and alienation is selfishness, the deepest reason for voluntary poverty is love of neighbor. Christian poverty has meaning only as a commitment to solidarity with the poor, with those who suffer misery and injustice. The commitment

is to witness to the evil which has resulted from sin and a breach of communion. It is not a question of idealizing poverty, but rather of taking it on as it is—an evil—to protest against it and to struggle to abolish it. As Ricoeur says, you cannot really be with the poor unless you are struggling against poverty" (ibid.).

6. See Dupont, *Les pauvres et la pauvreté,* pp. 38–40.

7. See ibid., pp. 41–45.

8. Ibid., p. 45.

9. "Comunicação pastoral ao Povo de Deus" prepared and approved by the Representative Committee of the National Conference of Brazilian Bishops, dated October 25, 1976, p. 16. We quote this document according to the reprint in the *Comunicado Mensal da CNBB,* October 1976.

10. Ibid., p. 15.

11. See above in Chapter 3.

12. "Comunicação pastoral, pp. 9–10.

13. Ibid., pp. 10–11. This quotation, as well as the one in the preceding reference, is taken almost literally from the pronouncement made by H. C. Fragoso, at the Sixth National Conference of the OAB (Brazilian Bar Association), held in Salvador, Bahia, from October 17 to 22, 1977. The text was published with the title "Advocacia: Igualdade e Desigualdade na Administração da Justiça," in *Cuadernos do CEAS* (Social Studies and Action Center, Salvador, Bahia) No. 47 (January–February 1977): 31–41.

14. For a more extensive consideration of this topic, also based on Paul's theology, see J. V. Pixley, "El Reino de Dios: ¿Buenas Nuevas para los pobres de América Latina?" in *Cuadernos de Teología* 4 (1976): 77–103. See also G. V. Pixley, *God's Kingdom* (Maryknoll, N.Y.: Orbis Books, 1981).

15. See SEDOC, May 1975, Col. 1083 ff.

16. See SEDOC, November 1976, Col. 465.

17. SEDOC, May 1975, Col. 1068.

18. SEDOC, November 1976, Col. 563.

19. SEDOC, May 1975, Col. 1102.

20. See SEDOC, November 1976, Col. 523.

21. See ibid., Col. 523 and 521.

22. See ibid., Col. 465–467.

23. See ibid., Col. 458, 460.

24. Ibid., Col. 473 ff.

25. SEDOC, October 1976, Col. 261 ff.

26. Ibid., Col. 262.

27. Ibid., Col. 262 ff.

28. Ibid., Col. 263. Concerning the transition from the consciouness of "the past" to the consciousness of "now" in the CEBs, see J. B. Libanio's study. "Uma Comunidade que se redefine," in SEDOC, October 1976, Col. 295–326, especially 297–306.

29. SEDOC, November 1976, Col. 570.

30. See ibid., Col. 478 ff. Here are two examples of the seriousness of this commitment, and of its consequences: "The conscious attitude of the evangelization groups toward these two problems (unions and land), based on faith and living experience of the gospel, are political attitudes which come into conflict with the ruling powers, as well as with the landholders, mayors, delegates, and union heads. It has reached the point where some farmers from the community have been arrested by the Federal Police because of their action related to the land problem. They clearly stated to the Federal Police the problems that the rural people are suffering, and gave witness to their faith and courage" (ibid., Col. 481).

"When five persons from the community were arrested by the Federal Police, the workers continued with greater zeal" (ibid., Col. 479).

31. See Bishop Moacyr Grechi, "Comunidade de fé e homem novo."

32. Ibid., p. 908.

33. See "Trabalho da Igreja Acre-Puruense em suas comunidades nos anos de 1974 and 1975" (mimeographed).

34. See Grechi, "Comunidade de fé e homem novo," p. 912. Also see, in the Bulletin *Nós Irmãos* of the Church of Acre and Purus, June 1975, p. 11, the interview with Sr. Antonio dos Anjos, a poor man sixty-eight years old who, since discovering the good news, has lived by preaching it and fulfilling it among the poor and abandoned, crossing rivers, highways, and roads to find them.

35. See SEDOC, November 1976, Col. 523. The most serious problem in the area is that of land, but it is not the only one. There are also other major problems demanding action from the Christians in the communities. For example, in the Experimental Station Community, the community leaders mobilized 200 people to exert heavy pressure on the public agencies to solve the water problem besetting about 600 families (see ibid.).

36. The Church has a very well established position regarding the squatters and the investors, based upon the law that is in force, whereby there is an attempt to serve the most defenseless people, guiding them, for example, by means of the various "catechisms" (Catechism on Land Rights, Catechism on Political Action for the Christian, Catechism on Social Guidance and Human Advancement, etc.). See in Grechi, "Comunidade de fé," pp. 916 ff, the points summarizing the guidance of the Church of Acre and Purus with respect to the squattters and the investors.

37. SEDOC, November 1976, Col. 533.

38. In the notes on these statements, the Council refers to 1 Corinthians 13:8; 3:14.

39. See GS 43. For a more intensive analysis of this topic, one may refer to Alvaro Barreiro, "Superação do dualismo entre fé e engajamento à luz da Constituição Pastoral 'Gaudium et Spes,' " in *A Esperança da Juventude é a Esperança da Igreja?* (São Paulo, 1976), pp. 81–96.

Chapter VI

1. We cannot resist the temptation to cite here two quotations from a great prophet of Christian hope, who has always come out in defense of the "downtrodden children." "The modern world has no time to hope, love, or ponder. It is the poor people awaiting their place who, exactly like the saints, are loving and atoning for us" (Georges Bernanos, *Les enfants humiliés* [Paris, 1949], p. 251). Precisely because "the modern world has no time for hoping," the hope of the world rests with the poor: "I say that the poor will save the world, and they will save it without wanting to; they will save it in spite of themselves; they will not demand anything in return, except knowing the price of the service that they have performed. They are doing this colossal thing, and of course they will not gain a penny from it" (ibid., p. 249).

2. Alois Müller, "The Poor and the Church: A Synthesis" in *The Poor and the Churches,* Concilium 104, p. 114.

3. See above Chapter 4, "Jesus, the Messiah of the Poor."

4. We can apply to this matter the comments made by Fernando Bastos de Avila, with respect to the challenge which hunger in the world represents to the

Church: "In this connection, the Church is in a privileged position to make an effective contribution. It is in fact present on both sides of the trench in both camps of the conflict. It is with those who are on the outside, the starving, the oppressed, whose needs and demands it can make explicit. It can be, and has been, the voice of those who have no voice of their own. But it is also with the affluent and the oppressors, whose consciences it can trouble with the voice of the oppressed. And it cannot abdicate from this mission without betraying its prophetic mission" ("The Church and World Hunger" in *The Poor and the Church,* Concilium, No. 104 [1977], p. 7).

5. See above, Chapter 3, "Biblical Grounds for the 'Privilege of the Poor,' " for the Old Testament, and Chapter 4, "The Gospel According to Luke and CEBs," for the New Testament.

6. See above, Chapter 3, "Theological Interpretation of the Status of the Poor in the Old Testament."

7. Gustavo Gutiérrez, "The Poor in the Church," in Concilium 104, p. 15.

8. Yves Congar, "Balizas de uma reflexão sobre o mistério dos pobres," in Paul Gauthier, *O Concílio e a Igreja dos Pobres* (Petrópolis, 1967), p. 271.

9. Eucharistic Prayer V.

10. See SEDOC, May 1975, Col. 1102.

11. In many CEBs there is a repetition of what Paul wrote to the Corinthians concerning the Churches of Macedonia: "We must tell you, friends, about the grace of generosity which God has imparted to our congregations in Macedonia. The troubles they have been through have tried them hard, yet in all this they have been so exuberantly happy that from the depths of their poverty they have shown themselves lavishly open-handed" (2 Cor. 8:1–2).

12. Comblin, "As Comunidades de Base," p. 465.